NOTHING WHATEVER TO GRUMBLE AT

BY JOHN REED

Sir Joseph Porter. HMS Pinafore.

JOHN REED

NOTHING WHATEVER TO GRUMBLE AT

His Story

AS TOLD TO
CYNTHIA MOREY

In collaboration with Nicholas Kerri
Book Co-ordinator David C. Neild.

Library of Congress Control Number: 2005909198
ISBN: Hardcover 1-4257-0256-2
Softcover 1-4257-0255-4

This book was printed in the United States of America.

To order additional copies of this book, contact:
Xlibris Corporation
1-888-795-4274
www.Xlibris.com
Orders@Xlibris.com

To order copies from the U.K. please phone 001-888-795-4274

29715

Contents

'Nothing Whatever To Grumble At'? . . . well, hardly ever! There are one or two grumbles in John's story, it's true, but the few you'll find pale into insignificance against his joy of performing in the Gilbert and Sullivan operas. But this book begins long before John's twenty-eight years with the D'Oyly Carte Opera Company; it starts with his happy childhood, and his early days in the theatre. And after the D'Oyly Carte, his amazing second career which spanned a further fourteen years as a freelance performer and director.

Cynthia Morey

FOREWORD TO JOHN REED'S AUTOBIOGRAPHY

When I was a youngster, the D'Oyly Carte Opera Company paid regular visits to our local theatre, the Golders Green Hippodrome, situated in a leafy suburb of North West London. The "patter man", as he was known, was John Reed, who had recently taken over the comic roles and who was to continue to play them for the next twenty years or so.

The D'Oyly Carte in which John Reed was so much the leading light, was an institution seemingly unchanged since Victorian times. Weekly touring throughout the year was interspersed with London season and tours to North America. It was an excellent company in the fullest sense of the word where nobody enjoyed top billing and all the soloists were treated equally. Nonetheless, it was natural for the comedian to be regarded as the star and in that role, John Reed was following an illustrious line from George Grossmith to Henry Lytton and Martyn Green. It is perhaps not entirely accidental that within a couple of years of his retiring from the D'Oyly Carte, the company itself had folded.

The "tradition" which is spoken about in equal measure with reverential respect and outright antagonism was, in fact, not quite the rigid chastity belt that supposedly had been imposed by Gilbert from the very start. Talented artists cannot be tethered to a fixed and mechanical way of performance. John Reed and his colleagues proved time and time again that they could perform the works of Gilbert and Sullivan without having to play them as shackled puppets.

Indeed it was because of the skill of these artists that the performances came up so fresh and sparkling.

Gilbert and Sullivan created characters that had instantly become part of the English persona and John Reed's nimble dexterity brought them vividly to life. It is hard to think of Ko-Ko, the Duke of Plaza Toro, Sir Joseph Porter or any of the other characters he played without recalling his own delightful style of performance. His rare and unassuming talent, his perfect timing and his great clarity of diction would have made him an asset to so many different facets of theatre. It is our good fortune that he happened upon Gilbert and Sullivan and the D'Oyly Carte.

Raymond Gubbay CBE
London August 2005

ACKNOWLEDGEMENTS

I wish to thank the following people, without whose help, this book would not have been possible.

My partner and Business Manager, Nicholas Kerri.

Cynthia Morey, for her unflagging enthusiasm and tenacity in writing this book for me. David Neild who, rightly or wrongly, persuaded me of the necessity for it.

John Fryatt and Melvyn Tarran who provided photos for the 'Grossmith Dynasty'.

And Jeremy Stevenson for providing historical documentation from his extensive archive.

And in this computer age, which baffles me, I would like to thank Peter Crichton and Jason Ellis for their technical help. Thanks also to Angie Arnell of the Gilbert & Sullivan Society for advance publicity.

This book, of course would not be possible if I hadn't spent so many wonderful years performing the works of 'Gilbert & Sullivan' and thereby made so many wonderful friends, my thanks go to them, and to my successors, who also endorsed the need for this book; Andrew Goodman, Richard Suart, Alistair Donkin and Simon Butteriss.

John Reed OBE

FOR HE IS AN ENGLISHMAN . . .

Some memories from former D'Oyly Carte Colleagues

VALERIE MASTERSON C.B.E.
(Principal Soprano)

At last we have the book we have all been waiting for, the biography of a fascinating man with an incredible talent. I cannot wait to read it.

John Reed has always had a very special place in my heart ever since I had the really great privilege of working with him so closely in the D'Oyly Carte Opera Company.

He is a man whose acting abilities and dramatic stage presence together with an impeccable sense of timing, sense of fun and equally of pathos, all rolled into one make him one of the most outstanding Savoyards in living memory.

I want to find out more about this genius and his beginnings so that I can know him a little bit more.

Being with John was always tremendous fun! Whether in 'digs' together, at parties together or on the stage together in *Iolanthe, Ruddigore, The Mikado* and the few performances of *Utopia Ltd,* we always had a good laugh. When we meet now or speak on the telephone, we still do!

JOHN AYLDON
(Principal Bass Baritone)

How fortunate can you get? It was my privilege to work with dear John for the first six years of my career, and I learned so much from his total professionalism – always inventive and fresh. What a generous colleague he was, too. Of course, I learned to love him dearly as a kind, funny and very special human being. Whenever we speak on the phone the years roll back, and I will always treasure him as my dearest friend – even if he does refer to me as 'the old bag'!

GILLIAN KNIGHT
(Principal Contralto)

When I was at school I played the Lord Chancellor in *Iolanthe*. Never, in my wildest dreams, did I think that one day I would conduct John Reed in that role – and I even played his train-bearer! Thank you, John, for all your wonderful performances. Knowing you and working with you has been 'a privilege and pleasure that I treasure beyond measure'.

DAVID MACKIE
(Chorus master and
Associate Conductor)

The first time I played Pooh-Bah in the D'Oyly Carte I was, to say the least, somewhat in a state of trepidation. The announcement that Kenneth Sandford was indisposed and the resulting groan from the audience was not calculated to instill much confidence in his already nervous understudy.

GARETH JONES
(Principal Baritone)

I managed to get through the first scene without any mishaps, but in the first dialogue with Ko-Ko I realised that I was giving him the wrong list of Pooh-Bah's titles. As every Pooh-Bah will know, both lists begin with 'First Lord of the Treasury'. The first list to Nanki-Poo ends with 'Lord Mayor' but the next ends with 'Private Secretary' so John Reed had to extricate himself from my confidently presenting him with 'Lord Mayor both acting and elect'.

John quickly replied, 'Lord Mayor would be very interesting, but suppose we say – as Private Secretary,' thus bringing the dialogue seamlessly back on course.

That little story sums up John Reed to me – an extremely generous performer who always put less experienced colleagues at their ease – a REAL star.

PEGGY ANN JONES
(Principal Soubrette)

'John's on the phone', my husband calls. Immediately I start to grin. The laughter of memories kicks in and I grab the telephone to talk to my dear friend. Inevitably we speak of our years together on stage, reminding each other of the hysterical events while performing the G & S operas, anecdotes of life on tour, and memories of the wonderful people we have known.

Recalling John and Cynthia's visit

to my cottage in Hertfordshire, and all three of us in fields nearby picking blackberries – all we heard from John was squeals of pain as he got entangled in the briars! The time we got bored on a rainy week in Edinburgh, and I bought some terracotta clay – and we spent happy hours modelling this sticky red stuff into unrecognisable items, much to the landlady's horror! Being trapped in my caravan for an afternoon in Oxford because two swans had decided to sit and snooze one yard from the van door, and every time we tried to step outside would hiss and flap their wings and attack us! We even thought we would miss the show that night – and John had only come over for a cup of coffee!

I remember John's support and encouragement when I first took over the soubrette roles, the wonderful rapport we had and the pure and simple enjoyment of working with such a warm, generous and talented friend. I would not have missed it for worlds, John.

PREFACE

The Grossmith Dynasty

George Grossmith

When WS Gilbert and Arthur Sullivan were casting their first full-length opera 'The Sorcerer' in 1877 (disregarding 'Thespis' – the short-lived collaboration presented as a Christmas entertainment in 1871) the two men were unknowingly creating the mould for all their future characters. There was the attractive young soprano, the soubrette, the elderly contralto, the dashing tenor, the bass baritone . . . and so on. And, above all, there was the 'patter' man – more difficult to find than any of the others. Sullivan noticed George Grossmith at a benefit performance of 'Trial by Jury' when he was playing a mere juror, and Gilbert later saw him in the part of the Judge. Both men agreed that he should be considered for the role of John Wellington Wells and Sullivan approached him, tested him vocally and decided that he would indeed be very suitable. Grossmith then proceeded to an interview with Gilbert at his house in The Boltons and read Wells's opening speech. The author was delighted, reassuring him that his voice, in spite of Grossmith's doubts, was exactly right for the part.

The proffered engagement to play John Wellington Wells in the new production of 'The Sorcerer' was not accepted at once. Grossmith, having worked as a journalist, had begun a successful career as a singer and entertainer, and had numerous profitable engagements in his diary – should he give these up for a new venture which might prove to be a failure?

Luckily for Gilbert, Sullivan and D'Oyly Carte, and for the launch of what would become the famous Savoy Operas, George Grossmith did accept, and never looked back. He became a star overnight, and was to prove one of their greatest assets. The parts he played are sometimes referred to as 'the patter roles' or the 'comedy roles', but they are perhaps most often known as the 'Grossmith roles' – a tribute to the brilliant little man who created them.

In 1889, during a season of 'The Yeomen of the Guard' George Grossmith left the D'Oyly Carte company after twelve years, to resume his successful career as an entertainer at the piano, both in this country and in the United States.

Walter Passmore

It was soon after this that Walter Passmore came upon the scene, taking over the Grossmith roles with great credit. He was an accomplished pianist and had toured with musical comedies and concert parties before appearing in 'Jane Annie' at the Savoy Theatre in 1893 with many of the regular D'Oyly Carte artists. This was a comic opera by James Barrie and Arthur Conan Doyle, with music by Ernest Ford, and resulted in Passmore's being chosen to create the role of Tarara in 'Utopia Ltd' later that year. He regularly played the comedy roles in the revivals of the Savoy operas, but appeared as Don Alhambra in the first revival of 'The Gondoliers' in 1898, the Duke of Plaza-Toro being then played by William Elton. When 'The Mikado' was given one of its many revivals at the Savoy in October 1896 after the mediocre run achieved by 'The Grand Duke', it reached its one thousandth performance. Passmore played Ko-Ko, and some critics considered his interpretation of the role to be superior to that of Grossmith. He was a better singer and a very accomplished dancer.

After leaving the D'Oyly Carte, Walter Passmore continued his stage career, appearing in many musical comedies, among them 'Merrie England' at the Savoy in 1902, in which he played the role of Wilkins.

CH Workman

In 1906 Mrs Helen D'Oyly Carte was once again at the helm of the Savoy Theatre, which had been let to William Greet for a few years. She began by putting on a revival of 'The Yeomen of the Guard' for which the cast list contained many new names among – these was C.H. Workman, who was to play Jack Point, Gilbert was very pleased with his performance. 'In Mr Workman we have a Jack Point of the finest and most delicate finish,' he is reported to have said. 'I feel sure that no-one will more readily acknowledge the triumph he has achieved in their old parts than his distinguished protagonist, Mr George Grossmith, and his immediate predecessor, Mr Walter Passmore.' It is interesting to note that back in February 1897 a comic opera was presented at the Savoy with no less than three of the famous patter men in the cast – one past, one present, and one yet to make his mark. The show was 'His Majesty' or, The Court of Vignolia by FC Burnand and Rudolph C

Lehmann, with music by Sir Alexander C Mackenzie. The three men were George Grossmith, Walter Passmore and C.H. Workman.

Workman would have been in his early twenties when he assumed the comedy roles with the D'Oyly Carte. He had hitherto created the small part of Hashbaz in 'The Grand Duke' and subsequently played a part in every one of the Savoy operas with the exception of 'Ruddigore', which after its original run in 1887 was not revived until 1921. On the retirement of Mrs D'Oyly Carte in 1909, Workman took over the management of the Savoy Theatre, but his real talents lay in performing and before long he was back on the stage. He died at sea, at the early age of forty-nine.

Henry A. Lytton

Next in succession came Henry Lytton, who joined the D'Oyly Carte in 1884, playing a variety of roles. After a brief absence from the company, he returned in 1908 and proceeded to establish himself as a great favourite in the comedy parts until his retirement in 1934. His debut with the D'Oyly Carte had certainly been unorthodox: he fell in love with a young actress, Louie Henri, while only seventeen, and still at school. They married almost at once, just as the new bride was about to set out on a tour of 'Princess Ida' with the D'Oyly Carte, and the two newly-weds decided that they could not bear to be separated. Louie was under the impression that the management was not in favour of married couples in the company, so the young Henry Lytton temporarily posed as her 'brother', obtained an audition, and was engaged at a salary of two pounds a week under the name of 'E.A. Henri'. The deception was soon discovered, the correct relationship accepted, and for his princely salary the young actor was required to understudy the part of King Gama. He did not get a chance to play the role, however, but three years later George Grossmith was taken ill and Lytton achieved great success when at short notice he stepped in to play the part of Robin Oakapple in 'Ruddigore'. Gilbert was so impressed by his performance that he presented Lytton with a gold-mounted walking stick as a token of his appreciation.

Henry Lytton was knighted in 1930 and died in 1936. His widow, Louie Henri (Lady Lytton) survived him and died in 1947.

Martyn Green

Martyn Green, Lytton's successor, joined the chorus of the D'Oyly Carte Company in 1922. He played some of the smaller parts before taking over five of the comedy roles. In 1926 he was transferred to the main company as understudy to Lytton, and six years later was playing Robin Oakapple in 'Ruddigore' and Major General Stanley in 'The Pirates of Penzance'. On Lytton's retirement in 1934, Green became the principal comedian, and was noted for his crystal-clear diction, unerring timing and lightness of foot.

In 1938 'The Mikado' was filmed, with Martyn Green as Ko-Ko and Sydney Granville as Pooh-Bah. A hectic schedule ensued, involving whole days at Pinewood Studios followed by a mad dash to the Scala Theatre, where the D'Oyly Carte were currently playing, for the evening performances. Fortunately the company's annual vacation was soon to begin, and life became easier. The film was given its premiere on January 12th, 1939 at the Leicester Square Theatre, but had a mixed reception, causing plans to film any more of the Savoy operas to be dropped.

The D'Oyly Carte company was disbanded when the Second World War broke out, but was soon on the road again when theatres were reopened after temporary closure. Martyn Green left to join the Royal Air Force, and during the war years his place was taken by Grahame Clifford, who soon became a favourite in his own right. After the war Green resumed his place as principal comedian and remained until the end of the company's Festival of Britain season in 1951. He was much admired in the roles he played and will be remembered for the many amusing pieces of stage business he introduced into the operas – notably his climbing of the scenery in 'The Mikado', which brought one of the biggest laughs ever. This innovation caused much dissention among the management, but eventually, with Rupert D'Oyly Carte's approval, it was allowed to continue.

After leaving the company in 1951 Martyn Green finally settled in America and followed a successful second career on the stage and in television. Even a very serious accident did not prevent him from continuing his work predominantly, though not exclusively, in Gilbert and Sullivan. He died in 1975.

All theatres were closed when war was declared on September 3rd 1939, and the forthcoming D'Oyly Carte tour was cancelled. When the government ban was lifted the company's first assignment was four weeks in Edinburgh, with Grahame Clifford as principal comedian, a position he occupied with considerable success throughout the war years. When Martyn Green returned in 1946 to take his place once more with the D'Oyly Carte, Clifford became a member of Covent Garden Opera. His vocal quality and versatility are illustrated by the variety of roles he sang. They include: Alberich *(The Ring),* Beckmesser *(Die Meistersinger),* Papageno (The *Magic Flute)* and Ping *(Turandot).*

Grahame Clifford

When Martyn Green left the D'Oyly Carte at the end of the Savoy Festival of Britain season in 1951, his understudy, Peter Pratt, took over the comedy roles, which he proceeded to play for the next eight years. He had joined the chorus in 1945, and was soon playing a number of small parts, later understudying and occasionally deputising in the roles he would later take over. But even before becoming the official understudy Peter had the chance to play several of the comedy roles when both Martyn Green and his understudy were ill. His performances no doubt impressed the management and influenced their decision when the time came to appoint a new understudy – and later – a worthy successor to the Grossmith roles. He left the D'Oyly Carte in 1959.

Peter Pratt

Peter Pratt was a very fine straight actor and went on to work extensively for the BBC. He also formed a group of singers who, under the name 'Music Mosaic', pursued a busy concert schedule, performing music from Gilbert and Sullivan and operetta.

So now we come to John Reed, a member of the D'Oyly Carte for twenty eight years twenty of them as principal comedian. With his dance training, impeccable timing, experience in repertory plus a pleasant light baritone voice, John had all the necessary attributes for assuming the Grossmith roles. He is the only principal artist in D'Oyly Carte history to have recorded all thirteen Savoy operas, and was awarded the OBE in 1977.

On leaving the company in 1979 John embarked on a whole new career in the UK and in the United States. He was in demand everywhere, from New York to Los Angeles and he was kept incredibly busy with some of the major opera companies. He directed Gilbert and Sullivan for thirteen years at the University of Colorado, where he was made an honorary professor. All these activities were interspersed with concerts and television appearances, both in this country and overseas.

John's career is a surprising and often intriguing story, and his contribution to the history of the D'Oyly Carte Opera Company as eighth in succession to the great George Grossmith will long be remembered.

A different King Gama

OVERTURE

I really can't remember which came first – the title or the book. When I was wondering what to call it, I thought of 'Nothing Whatever To Grumble At' with the addition of 'Well – Hardly Ever!' thus combining two of the operas, *Princess Ida* and *HMS Pinafore*. Then I looked back over all those wonderful years and decided that any complaints I might have had, though you'll come across them here and there, were as nothing compared with the happiness and fulfilment I'd experienced, so I cut out the extra words. Just 'Nothing Whatever To Grumble At' it remains. (In spite of this, I'm pretty sure that some of you more sceptical readers will be unable to resist muttering: 'What, never?')

The D'Oyly Carte Opera Company has often been referred to as a 'family' and that is how I shall always think of it. I can't remember when people joined or when they left – sometimes it seems as if we were all there together, at the same time. Once you became a member of the company, it seemed you were part of it for the rest of your life, wherever you went, or whatever you did afterwards.

My early days with the D'Oyly Carte are full of treasured memories, and it sometimes seems that these are clearer in my mind than those of later years. For many of us it was the beginning of our careers – we were young, enthusiastic and keen to do well. Cynthia was my first friend, and we found we had much in common – especially our sense of humour! Then there was Eric Thornton, one of the principal baritones, who had persuaded me to audition for this company I knew nothing about, and who performed operas I'd never heard of!

Many of the friends I met so long ago still keep in touch; Neville Griffiths, a principal tenor at that time, met and married mezzo Liz Howarth, and we still chat frequently on the phone. There were many weddings in the company over the years; Ceinwen Jones and Bert Newby (tenor, later company manager) married in New York on that first exciting tour of the States, as did Joy Mornay and Jon Ellison. Later, Beti Lloyd Jones married Mike Mackenzie (another tenor destined eventually for management.)

Sadly, Cei and Beti are now alone, but always game for a lengthy telephone session – the line is red hot at times. Then there was Valerie Masterson, one of the D'Oyly Carte's finest ever sopranos and Andrew March, flautist in the orchestra – they made a match of it too, and we speak often on the phone. Gillian Knight, the much loved principal contralto and Trevor Morrison, of stage management, were another pair united in the company, Christene Palmer, who followed Gillian in the 'Katisha' roles, and Norman Wright – I could go on and on . . . the Savoy marriage bureau seems to have worked overtime! Many other D'Oyly Carte folk, some from more recent times, of course, send cards, phone, or call in for a cup of tea (the kettle is always on) if they are in the area. But it is the friends I made in those early years who remain particularly dear to me and when we are lucky enough to meet, we fall into one another's arms, the years drop away and we are young again.

I started thinking about this book a long time ago, jotting down stories, anecdotes and oddments of information, until my eyes began to trouble me and I put it aside. Probably nothing more would have happened had it not been for a visit from David Neild, a tenor I had directed with the Harrogate Gilbert and Sullivan Society and the

Halifax Savoyards some years previously. He brought up the subject of my biography. 'John,' he said, 'This book *must* be written. People want it.'

I considered the idea afresh. Who could I get to write it? Then I realised that the very ones who could make this idea become reality were right there in front of me; Cynthia, who had written two books already, and knows me almost as well as I know myself, and my friend Nicholas Kerri, who over all these years had carefully kept every photograph and programme, and had assisted me on so many American assignments. Without his collection of important documents we should have had a problem putting this book together at all – had it been left to me, I should probably have scribbled recipes or shopping lists on the back of them and consigned them all to the bin! We even had a coordinator, David Neild, who offered to take on the administration and liase with the publisher. There was no excuse not to get to work.

And so the 'team' was assembled, and the book began to take shape. Cynthia made several visits to Halifax from her home in Oxfordshire, tapes flew back and forth and long phone calls were the order of the day. We had such happy times getting it all together and the whole process, instead of being a chore, turned out to be fun. We worked seriously most of the time but now and then something funny would turn up, there would be moments of sheer hysteria, and the kettle would go on for the fifteenth time. Friends who were keen to help sent photographs, and Peter Crichton gave us his invaluable assistance in processing them. I began to feel I would be repaying my loyal fans for all their appreciation and support. So many times, when I had been relating one of my stories outside the stage door, they would say to me, 'John, you *must* write this down!' Well, at last – better late than never – I am doing just that.

Now, just one note to all those academic Gilbert and Sullivan aficionados: Put away your reference books! This is no learned discourse on the Savoy Operas, but merely a light-hearted account of the joy of performing them, the camaraderie of fellow artists and the extraordinary things that can happen when you least expect them. In fact, it's just *my* story.

We hope you enjoy reading it as much as we've loved writing it!

John Reed OBE
Halifax England
Autumn 2005

. . . AND BEGINNERS!

CHAPTER 1

'Hallo,' cries the new-born baby-' (*Utopia Ltd*)

John Reed's Mother

My first appearance before the photographer.

My father, Bob Reed.

'Praise the Lord!' cried my paternal grandfather, falling on his knees in the middle of the street. He had been on his way to chapel when someone came running to tell him of my entry into the world. It was February 13th, 1916, right in the middle of the first World

War, and I'd arrived to join my three sisters, Christina, Betty and Anne, and to complete the family. The year of my birth saw Lloyd George presiding at Number Ten, and two future Prime Ministers born – Harold Wilson and Edward Heath. On a lighter note, two successful musical comedies were shortly to appear on the scene and lighten the wartime gloom a little. These were *The Maid of the Mountains* and *Chu Chin Chow,* the latter running for well over two thousand performances and starring Courtice Pounds, of D'Oyly Carte fame. Talking of the D'Oyly Carte *Principal Repertory* Opera Company, as it was then called, Henry Lytton and Bertha Lewis were well established in the comic and contralto roles respectively, and on my natal day they were performing in Holloway, North London. Decades later I was to live in that area, but never saw any sign of a theatre, so presumably it was demolished either by Adolf Hitler or developers.

My father was the butcher in the tiny colliery village of Close House, a few miles from Bishop Auckland, County Durham, as his father had been before him, and the rambling house attached to the shop is where I spent my happy childhood.

The Reverend John Lamb Reed, after whom I am named, was a Wesleyan Methodist minister – not, I hasten to add, in the least like the 'bigoted and persecuting type' referred to in *The Gondoliers,* but a gentle and honest man, much loved and respected in the area. The children adored him and followed him everywhere, sure of a kindly smile and a few sweets from his capacious pockets. During the war a stray bomb dropped right in front of our shop, making a small crater big enough, as my mother was heard to say, 'to hold a horse and cart'. Of course, it was only a fraction of the size of the bombs which fell in the second World War, but apparently powerful enough to blow out all the windows except that of my grandfather, and my sisters walked in their bare feet over a mass of broken glass without a scratch. Grandfather became a legend that day in our tiny village. He had taken no notice of the air raids, declaring, 'God will look after me,' and it seems that he was right. After that, whenever the warning sounded, everyone would hurry to get as close to him as possible, sure that they would be quite safe with Grandfather Reed.

But, gentle as he was, he was by no means always a quiet man, as I learned from a wonderful tale told by my mother. There were sometimes visiting preachers at the chapel, and on those occasions my grandfather would sit in the family pew at the front and listen to the sermon. One Sunday an extremely long-winded preacher was holding forth. He went on and on, and the congregation was becoming restless. At last he ground to a halt and announced the next hymn. 'We will now sing hymn number five hundred and eighty-six,' he said, 'Oh, for a thousand tongues to sing,' whereupon my grandfather's voice was heard to remark loudly from the front pew, 'Nay, lad, one like thine's plenty!' He had often been known to leave his seat during a visiting minister's boring sermon and go round to open all the chapel windows. They worked with a winding device, and the loud rattling noise that ensued would thoroughly disconcert the offending preacher and bring his tedious ramblings to a halt. When Grandfather himself was in the pulpit he would occasionally address any member of the congregation whom he considered was not pulling their weight with some such encouragement as, 'Come along now Mrs Jones, you can do better than that! Let me hear you raise your voice to God!' What a character – my great regret is that I was too young to get to know him. I'm told I was the apple of his eye. At school the other children used to tease me sometimes. 'You're called 'Lamb' because your father's a butcher,' they laughed. But I knew better. `John Lamb Reed' was my grandfather's name, and I loved it for his sake.

The village of Close House consisted of a few streets and half a dozen or so small shops, our butcher's shop being one of them. My father was the kindest, gentlest man imaginable, and wouldn't hurt a fly. So it's strange to think that he could kill a beast or wring a chicken's neck in the course of his work. I've known him to shed a few tears when any of us went away for a few days, even just for a holiday. But those tasks he undertook as part of his trade were something quite apart. His marriage to my dear mother was surely made in heaven, for there was such love and laughter in our house. I can't remember any arguments or cross words. Sister Anne was my elder by just four years; Chris and Bet, being several years older, mothered and spoiled me for all they were worth. I had the most wonderful childhood and have nothing but beautiful memories of that time.

Our house, joined as it was to the shop, seemed enormous to me as a child, with many large, high-ceilinged rooms. There were long passages, and a staircase with a splendid banister rail which curved excitingly in the middle – I remember sliding down this at every opportunity. Outside was like an enticing adventure land for me, with so much room to play in the huge yard, and lots of hiding places. There was a loft above the stables, piles of straw, a pothouse where father made sausages, polonies and potted meat, large wooden bins holding cowcake, a machine for cutting turnips to feed the cattle, stables for the horses. What a wonderful smell there was – I can close my eyes and smell it now, as if it were yesterday. Beyond the yard there was a further area with big gates leading into fields where cows and sheep were kept. And there were always animals around the house – calves, piglets, working dogs and guard dogs – the latter kept in kennels. I was allowed to have my own pet – a lamb, of course! There was also a pet pig called Billy, who had grown rather large, but was still vainly trying to get in through the back door.

Of course, in those days nearly everyone sang or played the piano, and our family was no exception. We would spend night after night round the piano entertaining ourselves and any friends or relations who might have dropped in. Ours was always an open house – anyone who called was immediately invited in for a cup of tea, and that meant cakes as well. Oh, those cakes! They were always homemade, and how well I remember mother's Christmas cake, with a piece of rice cake, a slice of cheese and a small silver coin on your plate. Christmas meant carols, of course, and the chapel choir would pass our house when out on their rounds and always return for the last carol. Everyone piled in, and when there was no more room downstairs they would sit all the way up the staircase. Cake for all, needless to say, plus ginger wine – nothing intoxicating for Methodists! So what? We never needed it. Everyone was having too good a time.

Talking of singing, mother had a soprano voice that I believe was something special. It had a quality which seemed to come straight from the heart, and heaven knows, her heart was big enough. She sang at many choir weekends, concerts, and oratorios with professional singers who had been brought from London. One day after a concert a couple of men turned up at our door carrying some strange equipment. They wanted to make a recording of a song which they had heard my mother sing the night before. Gramophone records were quite unheard of at that time in Close House, for the process was still at a very early stage. My father would not allow the recording to be made, but I do wish he had. If only I could hear that voice again.

I had piano lessons from Dr Dakin, who used to come to the house. He had already taught my sister Betty until she eventually out-played him and he could teach her no more. He did not have the same success with the rest of us, though we all played a little, and Chris and Anne could manage to thump out a hymn quite well. By the time Dr Dakin got to me, he was getting fairly old, and would drop off to sleep while I was struggling with 'The Blackberry Waltz' or 'The Fair Dance', with the family portraits jumping about on top of the piano. One day he woke with a start when I hit a wrong note. He took my hand and banged it on the right note. I got up, removed my music and went to my mother. 'I am not going in there any more,' I announced, whereupon she immediately went to see what had happened. Apparently old Dr Dakin had dropped off to sleep again, and I have no idea what went on or what was said. But I never had any more lessons from him, though I did not escape entirely. Mother was obviously determined that I should play the piano, so off I was sent down the street to a lady called Miss Peacock. This time there were no family portraits on the piano, but just a model of the Eiffel Tower which jumped about alarmingly as I pounded away. She didn't have much success with me either, poor dear, but at least I had some sort of foundation. This helped a lot later on, when I had to teach myself a song, or bang out my own line in a trio or quartet. But where music was concerned, Betty was the star. She was given her first engagement as organist at fourteen, and was a brilliant pianist who could have made music her career. But she – like the rest of us – (me included, believe it or not!) was very shy, and settled instead for a loving husband, a happy marriage and a family. Probably a good choice. Chris, the eldest, was simply content to be a housewife, and Anne, the youngest, became a school teacher. She married a young man who, after experiencing the trauma of Dunkirk, became a Methodist minister. Each of my sisters had a son, so I have three nephews.

Father, or 'Pop' as we called him, was really only proficient at one thing – his work. Mother, however, could turn her hand to anything – a legacy which she has, I believe, handed down to me. I tend to be impatient when engaging in any of my hobbies, always wanting quick results, whether it's painting, tailoring, or turning out endless intricate sweaters on one of my three knitting machines! And if I sow a packet of seeds I want to see flowers the next day – I just can't wait!

I should explain why we called father 'Pop'. It wasn't a version of 'Pa' as is usually supposed, but came from his habit of saying,

'Just pop upstairs for my glasses, honey,' or 'Pop to the shop for a packet of Target' (his favourite tobacco), 'Pop here,' 'Pop there.' So, 'Pop' he became. And what a dear man and affectionate father he was, devoted to his wife and family. An example of his kindness is illustrated in a story told to me in later years by my mother. She had taken me up to bed one night when I was quite small, and was listening as I said my prayers. 'God bless Grandma, Christina, Betty and Anne. Make me a good boy . . .' This particular night I had said all the usual things, then added, strictly off my own bat (if you'll pardon the pun) 'and please, God, sent me a tennis racquet.' Mother tucked me in, then returned downstairs, laughing. 'What do you think he's said tonight?' she asked father, then she told him of my request. Without a word to anyone, he got up, put on his cap and left the house. He went to the side door of one of the village shops (it was after closing time) and lo and behold – I awoke next morning to find a tennis racquet on my bed. Could anyone have a better dad than that?

CHAPTER 2

'But youth, of course, must have its fling'

(The Mikado)

Such was the freedom we had as children that any friends we made were immediately brought home and made welcome. I have since realised that this was probably mother's way of keeping an eye on the sort of people we were associating with! Looking back over those years it seems to me that there were always parties going on, either indoors, or outside in the spacious yard, which had a high arched section, the full width of the house. This was a perfect place for children to play.

I used to organise 'fetes', for which I charged an entrance fee of two pins, and devised all sorts of games and amusements. A clothes horse draped with a sheet made a fine tent for fortune telling. Then, for a couple of pins a child could climb a ladder to the top of a wall as high as the house, to which I had attached a rope. A thick walking stick was provided; you hooked the end over the rope, hung on, and swished down to the other end of the yard, where the rope was fastened at the bottom of the opposite wall. It was thought very thrilling – I called it 'the Aerial Flight'. Or you could be put in a barrel and rolled down the length of the yard, but it was very uncomfortable, so I only charged one pin for that ride. For the next exciting experience a swimming costume was necessary, and it cost a safety pin. A galvanised tin bath, pierced with tiny holes, was suspended from the ceiling, with a hosepipe in it. This showered a cascade of icy water straight from the cold tap on to the child beneath. I collected the pins from the enthusiastic participants, but never took part in this myself, though it proved very popular in the warmer weather. All this took place in father's pothouse, and I always ended the day with a lapel full of pins – what I did with them I can't imagine. Mother probably collected them for her dressmaking – a hobby at which she was extremely skilled.

The most exciting event of the day was the 'Sky Ride'. At the top of the archway Pop had the block and tackle fixed, and for several pins (this was the most expensive attraction!) you could sit in a leather loop attached to this contraption and be pulled to the ceiling. There you were fastened for a few minutes before being let down. It was very good value I thought, and there was usually a queue for this ride. Hannah Ingledew was the last customer one morning, and after paying her pins she was hoisted to the ceiling and fastened there. I was busy with another matter when mother called me for lunch, and I hurried into the house. Everyone else disappeared for their midday meals too, and I completely forgot about Hannah, who remained tied to the ceiling for the whole of my lunch break. I couldn't help noticing that she never came to one of my fetes again! There were many other amusements, but mother's tea and cakes were the highlight of the afternoon, and what was more important, unlike me, she did not charge!

I believe we had the very first car in the area – a twenty-four or twenty-five horsepower Ford, something I have never heard of since. It was actually a butcher's van, and the van section could be unbolted from the chassis and pulled up to the ceiling by block and tackle (yes, the same one used in the 'Aerial Flight!)'. Next, the `touring' section was lowered on to the chassis and securely bolted into position. This operation converted the vehicle into a family car, and off we all used to go at the weekend to the seaside, which was only about twenty miles away. How we loved that. During those excursions, travelling at perhaps twenty-five miles an hour, mother would say, 'Blow your horn, Bob, blow your horn!' whereupon Pop would reply placidly, 'I'm all right, Lizzie Ann!' (Why he called her that I really don't know, when she had a lovely name like Elizabeth). But Pop would never do as she requested and blow the horn, so mother bought one of her own – a great brass thing with a big rubber bulb. From that day on she would sit with it on her knee, hanging it out of the window and blowing it whenever she felt it was needed, in spite of father's protestations.

What a sight we must have been, driving along in that extraordinary vehicle, for during particularly busy times father would not have time to put on the touring section. My sisters and I would sit in armchairs in the back, with a piece of meat gauze between us and our parents, and pieces of the same material round the sides, partially obscuring us from the surprised gaze of passers-by. Mother would be poking that funny old horn out of the window and blasting away at every opportunity, while at the same time the rowdy din of some popular song would be coming from us in the back. Father would whistle and sing in a sort of grunting voice, and mother would add her fine soprano voice to the combined effort. What people must have thought, I really don't know, but what glorious times those were.

One of the bedrooms in our large old house was used as a playroom, and I remember an old rocking horse covered with real horsehide, and a big dolls house which opened at the front, revealing all the tiny furniture. Once I papered the small rooms with some wallpaper left over from my mother's decorating, not too successfully, for the floral pattern was so large that one rose covered an entire wall. My cousin Nancy and I would play for hours in that room, so engrossed that we hardly spoke a word. 'Post Offices' was one of our favourite games and I had stretched lines of cotton everywhere, on which had been threaded bobbins which would carry messages to all corners of the room. We would also play shops with this method of communication, pretending that the bobbins were the cylindrical containers which catapulted money and change to and from the cash desk in old fashioned stores. 'Change, Miss Witherspoon!' I would call, whizzing a bobbin over to Nancy across the line of cotton.

It was in that very room that I began my career in the theatre, for I built a stage, which in fact was a very large table, and of course there had to be a curtain, supplied by mother. Here Nancy and I performed 'The Princess and the Candlestick Maker' – all made up on the spur of the moment, and never the same twice, but oh, how I believed it all. Sometimes we performed this in the sitting room, which had a large bay window. This was excellent for a stage, for it had heavy curtains which worked better than those I had arranged in the playroom. I suppose most children do this sort of thing; life is all pretending when you are young – but I don't believe I ever grew up. At all events, I just had to continue acting until I finally made it my career.

There always seemed to be laughter in our house – even where other people might well have lost their tempers and had a row. Somehow we always managed to see the funny side of things. I well remember the day that mother decided to freshen up the kitchen ceiling with a new coat of whitewash – there was no emulsion paint in those days, of course. She intended to do it very carefully, so as not to splash the wallpaper, and had almost finished, when in came Pop. 'Whatever are you doing up there, honey?' he said in alarm, seeing her perched on a high ladder. 'I'm all right, Bob,' she replied cheerfully. 'Come down,' he ordered, 'You'll kill yourself! I'll finish it for you.' (There were only about two square yards to do). Famous last words! Down came mother as requested, and up went Pop. After one or two strokes of the brush he said, 'By jove, this is hard work, honey,' whereupon he dropped the brush. Placing the bucket on a shelf he went down to retrieve it, started to mount the steps again, bumped into the bucket and upset it over his head. Whitewash was everywhere, ruining the wallpaper, and covering father completely with the awful stuff. I thought my mother would die laughing, Pop too! That's how it was with our family – no cross words, no recriminations – mishaps like this were turned into hilarious incidents, to be talked about and laughed over for years to come.

Pop was certainly a one-off, no doubt about that. He'd been delivering meat one day as usual round the villages in his horse-drawn van and was just about to start on the homeward journey when the hunt went by. Everyone knew Bob Reed, of course, and called out greetings as they passed. 'Hello, Fred! How do, Bill!' shouted Pop in return, then one of the riders yelled, 'Come on, Bob – why don't you join us?' No sooner said than done – the butcher's apron was off, the horse out of the shafts and saddled in a trice, the van abandoned, to be picked up later, and there was Pop – galloping away with the rest of them! What a character he was.

Pop adored his horses and had a particular favourite called Jenny. One day mother was holding a meeting of chapel ladies, and just as the china teacups were elegantly poised, in walked Jenny to take part in the proceedings – quite a surprise for everyone when a large horse ambled casually into the sitting room.

When I started school at Eldon, only a ten minute walk from home, it was usually my sister Betty who had the job of taking – or should I say dragging me there, for I hated going. I was such a hopelessly shy child. I later went to school in Coundon, a little farther away, where I sat my scholarship for King James Grammar School in Bishop Auckland. Heaven knows how or why, but I passed the examination – and what is more, got very high marks. In those days, if you passed at a certain level you did not pay any fees; at a lower level reduced fees were charged. Otherwise parents were liable for the full cost of tuition. I recall being very upset at the beginning of my first term to be one of the few boys without an envelope containing the fee to hand to the teacher. I have always been extremely independent, and asked my mother why I could not take some money like other boys – was I receiving charity? She laughed and explained the situation to me. Goodness – perhaps I was a little brighter than I thought.

I enjoyed being at the grammar school, but unfortunately my stay there was destined to be curtailed. The General Strike was about to cast its grim shadow over our lives, and the miners were very badly hit. There were demonstrations and parades, protest marches to London, and scarcely any money about. Father tried to help all he could, driving round the villages with meat for his regular customers just as he always had. He kept up supplies as usual to the hard-pressed families, letting them run up big bills and drawing out his own money to try and make ends meet. By the end of the strike he was close to bankruptcy, but sure that he would soon be repaid by all those whom he had helped during those hard times. However, this was not to be. Whether they were ashamed or embarrassed I don't know, but instead of paying their debts, his old customers turned their backs on him and took their business elsewhere. This broke father's heart and resulted in a complete breakdown. My mother was a tower of strength at this terrible time. Tended by her and his devoted family, and helped by his good friend Dr Mason, who used to come to sit with him every evening and play cards, father gradually recovered.

Mother then took matters into her own hands and showed what a good businesswoman she was. Determined to see money actually coming over the counter – no more unpaid bills or bad debts – she took on a fish shop in Darlington, and we left Close House. At the time of our move, the new shop was doing no business at all, but not for long – certainly not if mother had anything to do with it. Straight away she sent us round all the streets in the area, delivering pamphlets which read: 'Fish Shop at no. 10 Mayfair Road under New Management'. So keen were my sisters and I to help our parents that we saw to it that no house was missed out, and to our delight the new shop slowly but surely prospered, and business grew and grew. I was transferred from King James to Queen Elizabeth Grammar School in Darlington, and soon settled in. By a lucky coincidence, Anne, who was training to be a teacher, moved to a college next door to my new school. Before long we were on our feet again. Things were definitely looking up.

CHAPTER 3

'My brain it teems with endless schemes . . .'

(*The Mikado*)

Our new business had a house attached, which was very convenient for us, and we lived there for some considerable time. However, when we were able to do so, we moved to a more attractive house within walking distance of the shop. There we spent a number of happy years, our usual enjoyment of life and Pop's irrepressible sense of humour having returned after the unsettling time we had all been through. I was growing up fast, and going to dances, as were all my friends. Some of these functions went on till two o'clock in the morning, and father would tell me it was much too late for me to be out. I used to say to mother, 'I'm going to a dance tonight – can I take the car?' She'd reply, 'Of course – just tell your father.' So I'd go and tell him, and he'd always say, 'You'll kill yourself, going to these dances!' Then I'd go back to mother and say, 'Pop doesn't want me to go.' 'Oh, take no notice of him,' she'd answer. 'Don't be silly – just go and get yourself ready.' I did as she suggested, and sure enough, as soon as I got to the front door, there was the car, already out of the garage, washed and gleaming, with father giving it a final polish. 'Now, take care, and drive carefully,' he'd say with a sly grin. That was the sort of affectionate treatment we all received, making us determined never to do anything which might hurt or upset those wonderful parents of ours.

Then came that dreadful day – September 3rd, 1939. The country was at war with Germany. My first wartime work was with the Auxilliary Fire Service, when I was permanently on call. If an air raid warning sounded during the night I would jump out of bed, hastily pull on my clothes over my pyjamas, leap into the car and drive as fast as possible to my station. There I attached a pump to the back of the fire tender, picked up a number of other firemen, and stood by for any emergency that might arise. Nothing dramatic occurred – we were only ever called to put out a few incendiary bombs – there were no really serious incidents. On one occasion in Richmond, Yorkshire, I was driving an enormous fire engine with all the crew on board, just outside the town. We were on a minor road when the siren sounded, which meant we had to get back to the station at once. I had to try to turn the great engine round in that narrow lane, but only succeeded in getting the beastly thing completely stuck across the road. The exhaust was jammed in a bank of mud at the side, exploding as loudly as a whole rank of anti-aircraft guns – I was waging my own private war up there in the Richmond hills, complete with most effective sound effects! As it happened, we were not needed, thank heaven.

All my friends were volunteering or being called up into the forces, so I decided to volunteer too. It was to be the RAF for me – I was going to be a pilot, nothing less. But my hopes were dashed – I did not pass the medical. The result of my examination said that I had a trace of sugar in the bloodstream. Mother of course was alarmed, so I went at once to our family doctor. He agreed with the report, but said the condition was so slight that it had probably been caused by 'emotional excitement'. I was prescribed various remedies, but decided not to take any of them. I felt perfectly healthy, so why should I? When my actual call-up papers arrived, I had to have a second medical, and passed A1. Just as my hopes of becoming a pilot were about to be realised, disaster struck once more. The powers that be had discovered the earlier results, and I was failed yet again. Gone were my dreams of Spitfires and Hurricanes, and those pilot's wings. It was a great disappointment.

I couldn't bear the fact that I was doing so little towards the war effort, and my attempts to rectify this resulted in my becoming an instrument worker at a factory in Letchworth, in Hertfordshire. Before ending up in this capacity I spent a miserable week in a tank factory, but complained so bitterly that I managed to secure my release and transfer to instrument work. I turned out to be very good at this, and was proud to be able to work to two-tenths of one-thousandth part of an inch. I was billeted with a charming family, a Mr and Mrs Slade, who looked after me very well. I remember becoming very friendly with a girl called Lillian, who worked in a ladies' dress shop. We used to go dancing a lot, and I decided to continue with ballroom lessons, which I had begun at the Winifred Boylan Dancing School in Darlington, and I continued until I had all my medals. I suppose these activities might have hinted at a future career on the stage, though at that time nothing was farther from my mind. But at least dancing was a welcome diversion from the daily work in the factory, and as the war neared its end I finally managed to get my release from my Letchworth job to return North. I had to take up work briefly in another factory, of course, but at least I was home, and settled back with my family.

In addition to dancing, I had also taken a few elocution lessons, travelling to a Miss Smithson in Stockton for the latter. I particularly remember 'warming up' at a lesson one day, and doing an exercise designed to loosen the jaw and relax the hands. Miss S. and I were standing facing each other and saying 'Yes! Yes!

Yes! Yes!' in rapid succession, and flapping our hands wildly at the same time. At that moment a startled window cleaner appeared outside, and nearly fell off his ladder at the sight of these two mad people carrying on in this crazy way!

My old dancing partner – Joy Badell

Darlington Operatic Society played an important part in my life, for it was there I met Joy Badell. She ran a dancing school and choreographed for the society. They were very lucky to have her, for she was actually a professional, who had toured with an act called 'The Three Redheads', and was in fact the first woman to join ENSA. She taught me tap, ballet and musical comedy dancing, and I taught her ballroom in return. I was also friendly with her husband, John Bishop. Their marriage had been rather a romantic affair, for John had been in the audience at one of her shows, and although he was engaged to another girl at the time, as soon as Joy came on stage he said to the friend he was with, 'I'm going to marry that girl!' And he did. Joy was always my partner in the shows we did with the operatic society, and though I shouldn't say so, I'm afraid we stole all the notices! She was a really wonderful performer.

Life was much easier for me now, as we had put in a manager at the fish shop, and I was free to pursue the theatrical activities which were becoming more and more important to me. I had a girl friend, Marjorie Cooper, who was a member of a dramatic group called the Kay Players, named after their founder, Kay Barrow, and we were going out one evening – to the theatre, I believe. She asked me if I would mind calling for her early, as she had to attend an audition for the Kay Players' next play. When we arrived it seemed that they were looking for a leading man, and they asked me if I would read the main part. (I wondered afterwards if Marjorie had arranged this!) The character was an actor and film star, and the play, 'Goodness, How Sad' was by Robert Morley. Thinking it just a bit of fun, I read for them, and was astonished to be offered the part. I needed some persuasion, but finally consented. After all, I told myself, Marjorie was to be in the play, and the others seemed a nice crowd. How I remember that part – I had to smoke a cigar continuously, and I swear I was green by the end of every performance. I became an enthusiastic member of the Kay Players, occasionally bringing props from home to dress the set. After one performance which my mother had attended, I remember her saying, 'Everything was so familiar, I thought I was at home.' And sure enough, I'd brought so many pieces of furniture from our house that she well might have been! Kay Barrow was a hard taskmaster, but a very good director, and I did many more plays with her. It's strange how one thing leads to another. While I was busy with the Kay Players, a man called at our house one day to ask if I would consider playing the juvenile parts in his repertory company, Keith James Enterprises, in Stockton. 'But you don't know what I can do.' I said in amazement. I've seen you make an entrance and an exit,' he replied, 'and that's good enough for me.' I thought at that time he must be out of his mind, but now I realise what he meant. The way an actor makes an entrance on stage is of paramount importance; he must make an immediate impact on the audience – failure to do so will leave him at a severe disadvantage and establishing his character will be that much more difficult. Apparently I had passed the test, as far as he was concerned, and to my surprise I joined my first professional company.

Pre. D'Oyly Carte days:
at home in Darlington

I did absolutely everything in my new capacity – not just the juvenile parts. I painted the sets and went 'on the book' prompting – we all did that if we had a minor role. I found it very easy to learn my lines, which was fortunate, for sometimes there were six or seven hundred speeches to memorise each week. We'd open the play on the Monday night, and on the Tuesday the scripts would arrive for the next week's production, so before we really had time to relax into our current roles, there we were, learning our new lines and rehearsing the play for the following week. That's weekly rep for you. One week the scripts did not arrive until the Thursday; the play was 'Love in the Mist' and I was to play Nigel, an enormous part, hardly ever off stage the whole night. After that evening's performance I drove home as fast as I could, intending to get something to eat, then sit up half the night trying to get the first act under my belt. Could I possibly learn that huge part by Monday? It seemed impossible. My parents were still up when I got in, chatting nineteen to the dozen as mother related all the happenings of the day, and rather loudly, for Pop was a little hard of hearing. I couldn't study while that was going on, I decided, for I could hear it all over the house. Perhaps if I went and had a bath they might have gone to bed by the time I had finished, and then I could go into the lounge and do my studying. Placing my script on the side of the bath, I turned on the hot water and went up to fetch my pyjamas and dressing gown. Imagine my horror when I returned to find the book had slipped into the soapy water! It was battered enough to start with, for those scripts were constantly hired out, and that particular one must have been to every repertory company in the country. All the pages were loose to start with, and now they were all floating in terrible disorder.

I was distraught – there was so little time, and we had to perform the wretched thing on the Monday. Luckily my folks had at last gone to bed, so I gathered up all those loose pages, took them down to the kitchen, switched on the iron and pressed every sheet dry. Then I sat up all through the night. I managed to memorise the first act by next morning's rehearsal, and impossible as it sounds now the play went on as usual on Monday. Events like this ensured that my time in repertory theatre was very exciting, and I can honestly say there was never a dull moment.

When I was engaged by Keith James, he took great pains to tell me not to reveal to the rest of the company that this was my first professional job. 'They don't like amateurs,' he said, 'and they're always annoyed when the local society take over the theatre for their show. They're out of work while the theatre is otherwise occupied, and they resent it.' So I never said a thing. Occasionally we would put on a play which needed a larger cast than Keith had at his disposal, and then he was obliged to draw the best talent he could find from local amateur sources. They came very willingly, eager for the experience, but often members of the regular company would be heard tut-tutting, and grumbling about working with non-professionals. I held my tongue – unknown to them I had recently been an amateur myself. Undoubtedly weekly rep was very hard work, but I hardly noticed, I was loving it so. Even learning all those lines was no chore for me; I seemed to have a photographic memory, for if I 'dried' during rehearsal I could close my eyes and see the printed words and their position on the page.

But tragedy strikes every family, and ours was no exception. Father, who'd been frail for some time – I don't believe he ever really got over the strike – took to his bed and died quietly and peacefully. My mother was beside herself with grief, as we all were, but the family all rallied round and were a great comfort to her. Realising the house was too big, and too full of painful reminders of happier days, we got together and bought a very nice bungalow, re-furnishing it in a modern style. Mother liked it, and was happy there – or as happy as she could be without my father. So life went on. Not long afterwards, having a couple of weeks free from rep, I was in town one day and bumped into Ron Thornton, the brother of a fellow I'd worked with in one of Darlington Operatic Society's productions. It had been 'The Duchess of Danzig' by Ivan Caryll – more of an operetta really, and I'd played the part of Papillon, a jester-like character. It's interesting to note, as I did long afterwards, that when the show opened in London in 1903, the Daily Graphic commented, 'The music often recalls the style of Sullivan, especially in the patter songs . . .' Well, well.

But I digress. Ron continued, 'Eric was here for the weekend – we were talking about you.' 'Really?' said I, 'What on earth about?' 'I don't know whether you know he's a principal baritone with the D'Oyly Carte Opera Company.' Well, I didn't know, neither had I heard of the D'Oyly Carte. But I tried to look suitably impressed. 'They do Gilbert and Sullivan,' he went on, 'and Eric tells me they're looking for an understudy for Peter Pratt, who plays all the comedy roles.' 'Curiouser and curiouser – what was Gilbert and Sullivan, and who was Peter Pratt?' Eric said, "I can only think of one man who would fill the bill, and that's John Reed." 'Would you be interested?' asked Ron. 'If so, I'll tell Eric. He might be able to arrange an audition.' I considered. An *opera* company? Me? And I was surprised that Eric remembered me, the show was ages ago. Still, it would be quite an experience to audition. So, 'Yes,' I said. 'Why not?'

Amateur operatic days, '*The Geisha*'.

CHAPTER 4

'Must have a beginning, you know' (*The Mikado*)

My audition with the D'Oyly Carte Opera Company was duly arranged, and Eric Thornton got in touch with me to suggest that I learn the Nightmare Song from *Iolanthe.* It would be a good audition piece, he said. I'd never heard of it before, much less the opera from which it came, but I bowed to Eric's superior knowledge and agreed to do it. Now, where could I find a score? Then I remembered someone I knew in Darlington, Raymond Bergin, who was very much in to that sort of thing. I had met him through a dear friend of mine, soprano Ada Alsop, who was much acclaimed at that time, both for broadcasts and concert work. Sure enough, Raymond was able to lend me a copy of *Iolanthe,* and I set to work. As a matter of fact I have that very score today, as I forgot to return it – a fact he reminded me of from time to time over the years till he finally gave up and told me not to bother. I learned The Nightmare Song fairly easily, in spite of the intricate lyrics, but then I had been committing so many words to memory rapidly over the past few years that I suppose it had become second nature to me. My experience in rep. was standing me in good stead.

My audition was to take place in Glasgow, though not in the theatre where the company were currently playing, but in a large hotel in Sauchiehall Street. When I arrived, there seemed to be dozens of hopeful applicants waiting, but I was called in almost at once, which was probably a good thing. There's nothing more nerve-wracking than waiting ages for your turn. I don't know who my adjudicators were, but no doubt Isidore Godfrey, the musical director, was there, and also Eleanor Evans, the director of productions. There were one or two other people, and of course the accompanist. The Nightmare Song went fairly well, I suppose – at least, there were no mishaps, and I followed it with 'Jack's the Boy', a number from *'The Geisha'*. When I had finished they gave me the standard answer: 'Thank you, we'll let you know.' 'Well, that's that,' I thought, not really caring, anyway. I'd booked into the Railway Hotel, intending to get back to Darlington as early as I could the next morning, and I decided to enjoy the rest of my stay. I thought I'd take in a show, and finding out that the ballet were in Edinburgh, I booked a ticket, completely ignoring the fact that the D'Oyly Carte were performing at the King's Theatre. I don't believe it ever crossed my mind to go and find out what Gilbert and Sullivan was all about. In retrospect, it seems strange that in spite of my family's love of singing round the piano, somehow strains of *The Mikado* had never been heard at number 38 Close House. I certainly made up for it in the future!

A week or so later, when all thoughts of the D'Oyly Carte had vanished from my mind, I received a letter from that company stating that they were now in Edinburgh, and would I be prepared to attend a second audition? It was now November 1951. Apparently Bridget D'Oyly Carte and her manager, Frederick Lloyd would be present this time, and the audition would take place at the Empire Theatre.

So off I went to Edinburgh, found the Empire, where this time only a few people were waiting to sing. I was the first to be called on to the stage, which was lit only by working lights. The auditorium was very dark, with a few dim figures scarcely discernible halfway back. I sang my two numbers as before, and was then asked to do some dialogue. I thought for a moment, then remembered a dramatic scene from a play I'd done with the Kay Players, called *Berkeley Square,* so I went into action. 'I'll show 'em,' I thought. The excerpt I'd chosen required me to dash wildly round the stage, threatening, screaming, and shouting at invisible creatures, 'Ghosts! Ghosts! You are all ghosts!' It occurred to me long afterwards that my outburst might have put them in mind of Act II of Ruddigore!

When I finally came to the end of my *tour de force,* there was a deathly hush. Well, Johnny, I thought – you've gone too far this time! I collected my music and was about to make my exit when the silence was broken by a disembodied voice from the auditorium: 'We want you, Mr Reed – how soon can you join us?' Stunned. I stumbled into the wings, to be confronted by a smiling Mr Lloyd. I explained that I would need a couple of months at least, being currently involved in a number of things. I left the theatre in a complete daze, clutching several scores that I had agreed to study, and made for the best hotel I could find. Tonight I would just have to go to see the D'Oyly Carte – there was no alternative now. In the light of my prospective engagement with the company I thought it rather strange that nobody offered me a ticket for the performance. But they did not, so I paid for one myself.

The opera that night was *The Gondoliers,* and I watched, fascinated, as Peter Pratt entered as the Duke of Plaza Toro. He was accompanied by Ann Drummond Grant as the Duchess, Shirley Hall as Casilda and, yes – there was Eric Thornton as Luiz. The whole thing seemed so stylised, so polished – could I do that? I wasn't at all sure. I particularly remember to this day how impressed I was with Leonard Osborn and Alan Styler as Marco and Giuseppe, and I suppose I enjoyed the performance. But what I was really thinking about was how would I fit into that company? Would I be doing the right thing if I accepted a contract? But, even more important – how was I going to tie everything up at home, and maybe find a suitable companion for my mother, who could not be left alone in her present distressed condition? She had never got over the loss of my father, and depended so much on me for everything. Well, at least I had a little respite – I could always turn down this offer – after all, I hadn't signed anything. Yes, that was what I would do. Just as I arrived at this decision and was feeling quite relieved, the phone rang, and it was the D'Oyly Carte office. The company would be in Newcastle in less than two weeks – would it be possible to speed things up and join them then? I don't know what happened, but in a weak moment I said yes, I would do it. If I had been able to delay things for two months, as I had expected, I never would have joined the D'Oyly Carte Opera Company. Fate is a strange thing.

I have to say that although my mother was so sad to see me go, I received nothing but encouragement from her. 'It's such an opportunity for you,' she insisted. 'You *must* go.' I was pleased and relieved to have been able to arrange a charming companion for her, who turned out to be just the right person. She was an ex-nurse, Miss Petitt, and the two of them got along wonderfully well. Needless to say, sad as I was to go, that was a load off my mind.

It was only a thirty-mile drive to Newcastle from Darlington, and in what seemed like no time at all I found myself in the Theatre Royal, surrounded by strangers; trained singers at that. What on earth was I doing there? That evening I walked about backstage, knowing nobody – I can't remember being introduced to anyone – and hearing all the principals 'warming up' before the performance. 'Minni-minni-me, minni-minni-me, minni-minni-me' down the scale came from Joyce Wright's dressing room, some booming contralto arpeggios from Ann Drummond Grant, and a lusty 'hip-bath, hip-bath' spanned the octaves from Alan Styler's room. Tenors blasted up and down the scale, and a soprano warbled somewhere up in the stratosphere. I'd never done a vocal exercise in my life. I suppose I'd have to see what I could do. To say I felt vocally inadequate was an understatement, though if I'd known then what was in the mind of W.S. Gilbert when he engaged George Grossmith as John Wellington Wells for the first ever performance of *The Sorcerer,* I'd have felt a lot better. It's worth recalling what passed between the two of them at that first interview:

It seems that Grossmith read the part of Wells and saw how excellently it would suit him, but said to Gilbert, 'For the part of a magician I should have thought you required a fine man with a fine voice.' 'That,' replied Gilbert, 'is exactly what we *don't* want.' Whereupon Grossmith went on to play all the comedy roles with enormous success. I wish I'd known about that. I needn't have worried so much about scales and arpeggios.

I was plunged into intensive work immediately, learning my understudy parts as a matter of urgency, and praying that Peter would remain healthy – at least until I was ready to go on. At the same time I somehow had to learn the chorus work too, and I was thrown on for this long before I was ready. I was also ordered to watch in the wings, which I hated, and sometimes from the front, which was a little better. But though I knew I had to conform, and reproduce the traditional moves and gestures, I did not want to become a carbon copy of Peter: I was an entirely different person, and would eventually want to play the parts my own way. At that stage of my career I had no thought of ever taking over those roles; I did not expect to, nor did I even want to.

John Reed and Cynthia Morey

The very first friend I made in the company was Cynthia Morey, who understudied some of the principal soprano roles. She had joined the previous March for the Savoy season, so had been in all the operas and knew them quite well by this time. We met at understudy rehearsals, had a few laughs, and found we had a similar same sense of humour.

Towards the end of my second week in Newcastle, I was putting on my coat at the end of an individual music rehearsal one day when Jerry Stephens, the stage manager, came hurrying in, and a whispered conversation took place between him, Bill Cox-Ife, who had been playing the piano, and Miss Evans, who had called in to tell me about the next day's call. I listened as hard as I could, while trying to appear engrossed in my scores, and heard the words, 'Muriel Harding', 'Lost her voice', 'Can't go on tonight', 'Miss Morey' etc. I thought they'd probably go on like that for ages, and the best thing I could do would be to pop round to Cynthia's digs and break the news so that she would have a bit more time to prepare for going on for Muriel that night, for it was *The Pirates of Penzance* and Mabel was a big soprano role. Luckily I found Cynthia in, and she was very pleased to have the advance warning, and grateful to me for coming round to tell her. All seemed to go very well with the performance that evening and I suddenly thought – goodness, that might have been *me,* on for Peter! I applied myself to learning the parts even more assiduously after that.

Miss Evans, alias 'Snookie', alias Mrs Darrell Fancourt, wife of the principal bass baritone who played the Mikado, Pirate King etc, taught me the moves at some rehearsals, but at other times I was coached by Billy Morgan. He had been in the company years before as understudy to Martyn Green, then had to make way for Peter Pratt. I presumed that if Peter had been off before I was ready to take over, Billy would have had to go on. Now he was having to teach yet another new understudy to take the place I presume he considered to be rightfully his. I discovered that he had joined the D'Oyly Carte in 1920, so may have done some service during the first world war in which case he would probably been in his mid-twenties then, possibly even older. He was somewhat portly when I met him in 1951, and it would have been hard to imagine him as Robin Oakapple or Jack Point – maybe the Lord Chancellor or the Major General, but none of the other roles. I could sense his resentment towards me, and I was aware of a slight hostility in his attitude. But worse than that, Miss Evans would teach me a certain move or piece of business, and Billy would tell me something entirely different. This became so confusing that I was obliged to tell Miss Evans I could not possibly go on in this way. 'The trouble is, Miss Evans,' I said, 'Billy tells me to go one way, and you tell me the opposite.' The result was that I never rehearsed with him again, which was a great relief, for there was much to do, and time was short. Soon after this he left the company, which meant that the responsibility for understudying Peter was solely mine.

I had enormous help from everyone; Mr Godfrey (whom we all called 'Goddie'), Bill Cox-Ife, and of course Cis Blain, who ruled the wardrobe with a rod of iron, and who always made sure that my understudy costumes fitted well and looked right in every detail. Now the rest was up to me.

CHAPTER 5

'That's how I'd play this part' (*The Grand Duke*)

A month or so after I had joined the company, I was staying in some very dreary digs in Leeds. One morning, having tried unsuccessfully to get into the rather squalid bathroom, which seemed to be permanently occupied, I decided to go to the theatre and try the bathroom there. So I threw on some clothes and proceeded to the Grand, where the prospect of warmth and loads of hot water was very inviting. I was met at the stage door by Jerry Stephens, in a panic, 'You're on tonight,' he said, 'Mr Pratt's ill!' 'Ha, ha!' I laughed, refusing to believe what I heard, 'Pull the other one.' 'It's true,' said Jerry, 'You're to go to rehearsal at once.' It was *Ruddigore* that evening, and I was rushed off to a dingy church hall to rehearse the part of Robin Oakapple, unwashed and unshaven. I'd never felt less like rehearsing and going on, and would have given anything to return undisturbed to my Daily Telegraph crossword. All the principals had been called; Shirley Hall was my Rose Maybud, Leonard Osborn, Richard, and Fisher Morgan was playing Sir Despard. Somehow I got through the rehearsal, for I was fairly confident of words and moves by now, but the rest of the day passed in a daze.

All an understudy can do at a first performance is to say and sing the right words and be in the right place, or so it seemed to me. The productions of the operas were so firmly set that any unfamiliar move could 'throw' a fellow artist. There was no room for any variation, and Gilbert's dialogue was, as it should be, sacrosanct. Accustomed as I had been to the flexibility and occasional approximation of the script in weekly rep, this was quite new to me. It seemed that I coped satisfactorily, but I had no time to reflect on my performance of Robin, or analyse and learn from that evening's experience. I was informed that I should be playing Ko-Ko in *The Mikado* the next day, and would be rehearsing at ten am.

The following morning I was rushed through the rehearsal, and finally escaped back to the theatre to collect my thoughts and check costume and props. I was in for a shock. There were no personal props available for me to use – no trick fans for the 'Here's a how-de-do' encores, not even the horn rimmed glasses Ko-Ko traditionally used to read the Mikado's letter. All had been locked away.

I wondered what on earth I should do, then realised I had no option; instead of spending a quiet afternoon going over my lines, I must set to work with cardboard, paint and glue to construct the necessary fans. It was fortunate that I was good with my hands and could turn them to almost anything. I even had to go to Woolworths to buy a pair of glasses and knock out the lenses. I learned something that day which I have never forgotten. I vowed that if I ever became a principal I would make sure that my understudy had access to any of my props that he needed, and all the help I could give.

I was confronted by another disconcerting situation a year or so later, when the company were playing Norwich, and I was called upon in my understudy capacity to go on for the Lord Chancellor in *Iolanthe*. The Theatre Royal is a very old theatre, and the dressing rooms were in those days rather primitive. In the usual course I would have used the principal dressing room, which I was led to understand had been equipped with extra lights. Apparently the lighting provided had been quite inadequate, consisting of not much more than a couple of hundred watt bulbs. Putting on a character make-up as required for the Lord Chancellor would have been well nigh impossible under those conditions. Imagine my surprise when I entered the room and found that all the extra lights had been removed, and were nowhere to be found. It was pretty well impossible to put on any make-up in the resulting gloom. Robin Gibson, who was then Director of Productions, came into the room and was as incredulous as I. 'This is hopeless. I shall dress in the small part room, as usual', I said, gathering up my things and climbing the stairs. My companions were amazed when they heard what had happened. An understudy's job is hard enough without having to cope with any additional complications.

But, back to my first performance of Ko-Ko. Once again I was mainly concerned with fitting in to the performance as neatly as I could and remembering words and business. An understudy is always aware of the disappointment inevitably felt by the audience when it is announced that the actor they expected to see is indisposed, and that his part will be taken by someone else. So there is that feeling to overcome before winning them over, and it could be quite a struggle in a company like the D'Oyly Carte, where principals stayed long enough to become favourites with the audience. Of course, I thought nothing about that during my first performance as Ko-Ko, and had no idea how I had done when the curtain finally came down at the end *of The Mikado.* What I do remember is that one of the chorus ladies, contralto Barbara Wells, came up to me after the show and said, 'Oh, you were so sweet. I wanted to mother you!' I would certainly have been glad of a bit of mothering just then, and told her so, and since that day I always had a 'stage mother'. Barbara left the following year, and Beti Lloyd Jones became my new 'stage mum', a position she held until I left the company in 1979. After I took over the roles from Peter in 1959 she would always come to my dressing room before the show, wish me luck and fasten my Lord Chancellor's collar or roll up my 'little list'. In fact it became such a ritual that I almost couldn't go on without the nightly visitation – we theatre folk are a superstitious lot! Then she'd give me a kiss, say, 'Good luck, son,' and rush away to get ready herself. Beti first assumed her duties in Oxford, so of course we had to commemorate it every year with 'Mum's Day', when she would receive a card and a gift! On one occasion Beti was off after quite a serious car accident, but she still managed to phone me from the hospital to perform her 'maternal duties' verbally.

Over my eight years as Peter's understudy I occasionally played all the comic roles, and in the early years rehearsed regularly with 'Snookie', till I was confident that I knew them thoroughly. Many of the company were rather scared of her; she had large dark eyes which could intimidate, scorn or ridicule the unfortunate recipient of one of her famous glares. I remember a rehearsal in Southsea when she was at the end of her tether. Donald Adams was also learning the bass baritone roles he was understudying and would eventually take over from Darrell Fancourt. He was making all sorts of mistakes, which was upsetting Snookie and I could see she was losing her temper. When I made my entrance I turned the wrong way – or so she thought. Now I knew she was in the habit of changing her mind about moves, and I had made a point of always writing them down so that there could be no argument. On this occasion I heard her give an exasperated 'tut-tut' – something I cannot stand, so I stopped in my tracks. 'Just a minute, Miss Evans,' I said, 'I have only had one other call on this. Words and music I can forget, but moves – never!' Then came the tears. 'Well, we'll just have to have more calls,' she said, and we carried on. I was so angry that I wouldn't meet her eyes, which was quite difficult, for she was never more than a couple of feet away, following me wherever I moved. This went on for several days, and created a dreadful atmosphere, till one day I thought to myself, 'This is getting me nowhere – I can't go on working like this' So the very next day she arrived looking particularly smart. 'Oh, Snookie,' I said, 'What a lovely hat.' 'Do you like it darling?' she replied, and after that we were friends again, and the atmosphere was back to normal. 'Oh, well,' I, thought, 'it was worth a lie.' I hated that hat.

There were several small parts which principal understudies played as a matter of course, and I particularly remember being issued with a terrible smock and broad-brimmed hat for the Second Citizen in *The Yeomen of the Guard.* I only had a few lines to say, just after Jack Point's entrance. Then there was Annibale in *The Gondoliers,* another speaking part in the second act; neither of these roles taxed my dramatic abilities very seriously, though I would be the first to say that the smallest of parts in the Savoy operas must be played as well as they can be. Donald Adams had been playing Antonio in the opening of *Gondoliers,* but when he became a principal the part passed on to me. It's a small but quite important role, full of energy and joie de vivre, and requires nimble feet for the little dance across the front of the stage that occurred in the production of that time. Antonio's song, too, 'the merriest fellows are we' contributes significantly to the general gaiety of the opening scene, and I used to enjoy that.

Later on, in 1955 I was to inherit the part of the Learned Judge in *Trial by Jury* on the departure of Fisher Morgan, who had been playing it up till then. You couldn't have found two more different characters; there was he, a big, sonorous baritone who had been playing the Pooh-Bah roles, and I – with the lightest of voices more suited to capering about as Ko-Ko. However, I pondered on this, and decided to play the judge with a twinkle in the eye, and a mischievous sense of humour, which seemed to work for me. Now and again funny mishaps can occur on stage, and I recall a performance of *Trial* one night when I made my entrance, got to the Judge's chair, and instead of singing, 'For these kind words accept my thanks, I pray' I opened my mouth and sang, 'For these kind words we thank the Lord for thee,' much to my own and everyone else's surprise. I don't know where those words came from, but maybe Reverend John Lamb Reed, my Methodist grandfather, had decided to put his oar in.

Going on for Peter always terrified me even when I was given ample warning. I would receive a letter from the office, saying, 'I would like you to play Jack Point, Bunthorne, (or whatever) in your capacity as understudy on such-and-such a date,' signed 'Bridget D'Oyly Carte'. Even when I was given adequate notice, I was very nervous – still am, I suppose, though as soon as I am on stage I am quite all right. My first Bunthorne was at the Memorial Theatre, Stratford on Avon, a matinee performance, and I went as a matter of course to number one dressing room, which would be mine for that afternoon. I needn't have bothered – the room was locked and the key had been taken away. The management did offer me Fisher Morgan's room, as he was not involved in *Patience,* but I declined. I played my first Bunthorne from the chorus men's dressing room, as I had in Norwich. Such behaviour as this was beyond my comprehension.

The role always allocated to the principal comedian's understudy was Major Murgatroyd in *Patience*. *This* allowed quite a lot of scope for individual characterisation, though I was still very much aware that I was the third member of a trio, working closely with Colonel Calverley (Darrell Fancourt, later Donald Adams) and the Duke of Dunstable (Leonard Osborn). At one performance, after the 'Now is not this ridiculous' double chorus in Act 1, Darrell strode across the stage to say, 'Angela! What is the meaning of this?' but somehow got caught up in his spurs. He would have had quite a fall had I not managed to catch him just in time and there might have been a nasty accident. Nothing daunted, he said to me in a loud stage whisper, 'Ha, ha! Nearly went arse over tit, then!' Of course, these words were perfectly audible to the audience, who roared with laughter. Darrell's 'asides' were often louder than some people's normal dialogue, and constituted an important part of his characterisation, in that they never varied from one performance to another – apart from the occasional unexpected incident like that, of course.

From 1957 to 1958 I played Cox in the one act three-hander *Cox and Box,* with Frederick Sinden as Box, and George Cook as Bouncer. It was the only piece with a libretto written by FC Burnand, and not WS Gilbert. We had a lot of fun with this – you couldn't help it – but there was quite a scramble to change during the interval, as it was always part of a double bill, and usually followed either by *HMS Pinafore* or *The Pirates of Penzance,* in which we were all involved in the opening scene.

When I was still quite a new member of the D'Oyly Carte and had just learned the part of the Major, there was a full company call to put me into the show. The 'love-sick maidens' were standing by, waiting for their entrance, and one of the principal ladies, indicating me, remarked loudly to another, 'They do get some silly asses for these parts, don't they?' This comment was reported to me, and of course I was very hurt. But now I just see the funny side of it. After all, this 'silly ass' lasted for twenty-eight wonderful years.

Cox & Box

CHAPTER 6

'A dark and dingy room in some back street . . .'

(*HMS Pinafore*)

A contract with the D'Oyly Carte normally ran for a year, with approximately forty-eight weeks of performances and a four week break. It usually included a London season, either at the Savoy or Sadler's Wells, or occasionally at the Shaftesbury (then the Princes) Theatre or the Saville. There were many months of touring, and in 1951, when I joined, it meant fortnightly train calls taking up the whole of Sunday – your one free day. What an extraordinary company it was! Carriages were reserved for us of course, but compartments were labelled, 'Principals', 'Ladies of the Chorus' 'Gentlemen of the Chorus', 'Orchestra', 'Stage Management', 'Wardrobe' etc, and we were expected to travel like this, sometimes on journeys which lasted six hours or more. By this time Cynthia Morey and I had become great friends, and usually spent our spare time together. When it came to those long dreary train calls we certainly didn't want to travel in separate compartments, and I believe we played quite a part in getting the rigid rules relaxed and all the unnecessary segregation stopped.

Once, during a three-week run in Edinburgh, it seemed to rain the whole time, and we took up oil painting. We painted canvas after canvas, and when it was time to move on we managed to grab a whole compartment to ourselves and staged an art exhibition, putting ridiculous prices on each masterpiece. Needless to say, we didn't sell any, but we had a great time, and it certainly relieved the monotony of the journey. Cynthia was always full of ideas – indeed I like to think we sparked each other off with ideas for special birthday cards which we made and painted for members of the cast. With such a large company birthdays and anniversaries were always cropping up, and we never missed a chance to produce something funny (or occasionally rude!) to make everyone laugh.

Painting was a good hobby to pursue on tour, being reasonably portable, but some of the activities I indulged in were rather more difficult to transport by train. I became interested in tailoring, and made all sorts of fancy waistcoats, trousers, and even a sports jacket, of which I was very proud. The next thing was rug making. I had watched a demonstration of a machine in a department store in Newcastle – it was Binns, I think – and became fascinated. 'I can do this,' I decided, looking at all the beautiful rugs made so easily by this gadget. I had to buy it, and all the necessary wools to go with it, and I was soon working away in the digs.

Some time later I decided to travel by car – one or two people had started to do this – and of course life became much easier. Hobbies were no longer a problem, and later on I bought a knitting machine from which poured endless sweaters. After the regimented train calls it was a joy to start out when you wanted to, and stop on the journey if you wished. And no more queuing for taxis at each end, either, just door to door comfort. I must admit, though, that my Ford Popular had rather primitive heating, and on one particularly cold day when Cynthia and I set out from my home in Darlington, my mother insisted on providing us with hot water bottles for the journey.

Much has already been said about theatrical digs, and many are the tales that have grown out of all proportion over the years. But some of those I stayed in need no exaggeration, and are a legend unto themselves. The D'Oyly Carte used to advertise for accommodation a few weeks before we were to arrive in a town or city, and the replies received would be put on the notice board at the stage door. During the performance an announcement would be given over the tannoy. 'Digs letters for Manchester, Edinburgh, Birmingham (or wherever) have arrived'. As soon as ever we could, we would rush to the stage door, pushing and shoving to try to get the best ones. Letters would be snatched, glanced at, put back or kept for further scrutiny, 'Here's one for two girls,' one of the boys would shout, and 'Two doubles, no animals' called someone else. There was a lot of laughter, and plenty of rude remarks. Cynthia seemed to have the knack of picking just the right letter, and invariably did very well. It was not at all unusual for her to find digs with full board for thirty-five shillings a week – I don't know how she did it. We were on very low pay, of course, though I had just received a rise of two pounds, bringing my salary to a startling eleven pounds a week. Out of this I had to run my car, so I was always glad to get some reasonable digs, and more often than not the cheaper ones were the best.

I particularly remember Mrs Mack's in Belfast. 'The higher you go, the cheaper it is,' she announced in her wonderful Irish accent as we filed into the hall. I was nearly knocked flying as Cynthia and Alice Hynd rushed past me, making for the attic. I ended up with a bedroom on the first floor, probably five shillings a week more than the girls', but I did have a wardrobe, whereas they had to make do with an old grandfather clock from which the works had been removed and a rail put in. Mrs Mack was very kind, and she did make us laugh. She liked her 'little drink' every evening, and would cross the road to the pub opposite, returning later by taxi. It was hilarious to see her staggering into the cab at one side of the road and tumbling out on the other. Cynthia, Alice, Johnny Fryatt and myself would try to get into digs together, for when we did, laughter was guaranteed. Alice, from Coupar Angus in Perthshire, who had one of those rare voices – a true contralto – had joined the company a few weeks after myself, with soprano Lorna Pobjoy. John Fryatt arrived on the scene a few weeks later, so we were all busy learning our chorus parts sometimes late into the night. There was a time in digs in Harrogate when all four of us were singing away after supper, and the landlady knocked apologetically on the door, saying, 'Your music is so nice – but would you please keep it for the morning?' It was probably already well into the morning by then, but we were so engrossed that we hadn't noticed.

It's extraordinary to look back now at the living standards we had to endure on tour in the fifties. We'd come from warm comfortable homes to digs that were often unheated, beds that were sometimes damp, and rules and regulations that were hitherto unknown to us. Tepid baths were available once a week at some establishments, and then at a shilling extra. But we survived, and I don't remember any more colds and sore throats than we have now. Most of these theatrical digs have long since disappeared, but many of those landladies were the salt of the earth, and did all they could to make us comfortable. Maybe there was no central heating, but often a roaring fire would greet us when we got home from the theatre, and we received much kindness from them, and would return again and again. On one tour I had a bedsit on the first floor of a house in Leeds where the dear old landlady used to carry my meals upstairs. 'Oh, Mr Reed,' she remarked one day as she puffed upstairs carrying a tray, 'I'm so tired – I could just fall prostitute on that bed.' Julia Goss also told an amusing anecdote of some Leeds digs. She had a charming landlady, and very comfortable accommodation, but breakfast was at eight-thirty am which Julia found a little early. After a few days the landlady enquired whether everything was satisfactory. 'Oh, yes,' said Julia, 'but there's just one thing – breakfast is a little early for me. You see, we work rather late, and I do like a lie-in in the morning.' 'Oh, that's no problem at all, my dear,' was the reply, 'You can have breakfast at any time you wish.' The next morning Julia came down to breakfast at about eleven o'clock. 'Did you have a good sleep?' enquired the kind landlady. 'Oh yes, thank you,' replied Julia, 'It was wonderful to be able to sleep on a little longer.' 'That's good. I have your breakfast all ready for you,' said the good lady. 'I've been keeping it warm.' And that is just what she had done. She'd boiled the egg at the same time as usual, and it was all prepared on a tray. She was so eager to please, so what could poor Julia say except 'Thank you,' and carry on with her two hour and four minute egg!

I shall never forget the day Alice Hynd took poison in the digs in Glasgow – I hasten to say that it was by mistake! It was fairly early in the morning, and, half awake, she sleepily swallowed a large amount of hair tonic instead of the linctus which had been prescribed. Clearly marked on the bottle was 'Not to be taken internally', and clutching her burning throat, she realised too late her mistake. Poor Alice shrieked out, waking Cynthia, who was sharing the room. 'Look what I've done!' she croaked, whereupon Cynthia, horrified, leapt out of bed in a panic. Rushing to my room, she pounded on the door, shouting, 'Alice has taken poison!' To say I woke with a start is an understatement. On hearing this terrible news I jumped out of bed, threw on some clothes over my pyjamas, and without stopping to ask any questions I rushed Alice off to hospital. Along Sauchiehall Street we raced, hardly noticing any traffic lights and never relaxing until our patient was delivered into medical care. Afterwards, when all was well, we saw the funny side of the situation, for in the midst of all the panic our landlady had appeared with plates of bacon and eggs, and calmly asked, "Won't you have your breakfast before you go?" Best of all, a paragraph appeared in the Glasgow paper the following day entitled, 'Opera singer takes poison' – Alice certainly knew how to grab the headlines!

One year – it would have been 1953 – we were due at the New Theatre, Oxford in late May, and Cynthia had the bright idea of renting a houseboat instead of looking for traditional digs. We wrote to some magazine or other, which resulted in a hilarious fortnight on the 'Buttercup', moored at Iffley Lock, a couple of miles from the town centre. The weather was good and the river was warm enough (or nearly) for swimming. Accomodation was fairly primitive, and I shared a sort of shelf with John Fryatt, who had a nightmare one night and tried to push me out of the window. However, the experiment must have been successful, as the following year we opted for a boat again and stayed in a large converted landing craft moored at Port Meadow. Alan Styler, who played many of the light baritone roles, and a couple of others – had a rather rickety houseboat further along the bank. Apparently it was not suitable for fishing there, so it was not unusual to wake up and see two legs dangling down in front of the window as Alan tried his luck from our roof.

I suppose my days in the chorus were the happiest time I spent in the company. The people one joined with always remain rather special, and although they left and went their separate ways, they are always part of the D'Oyly Carte family. Cynthia became a principal in 1954 and left in 1957 to do other things in the theatre, but we have always kept in touch and always will.

Theatrical digs gradually became fewer and more difficult to find, and we found guest houses impersonal and inconvenient, and hotels too expensive, then Peggy Ann Jones hit on the bright idea of touring in a caravan. This was much later on, in 1969, and it wasn't long before some more of us followed suit. Peggy had joined the company in 1958 and was soon playing small parts and gradually taking over more of the principal soubrette roles.

There was quite a crowd of us travelling with our caravans, booking sites in advance, and taking part of our home with us – dogs as well, in some cases. I was able to take my beloved boxer, Sheba, with me, and she was great company. Pauline Wales, Tom Lawlor, Brian Sharpe, Colin Wright and Philip Potter were among the D'Oyly Carte 'travellers' and a great camaraderie formed between us. I have always described the company as a large family; living and working in such close proximity formed a bond that seems to grow even stronger with the years.

John with 'Sheba' on tour

CHAPTER 7

'They sing choruses in public . . .' (*Ruddigore*)

I was 'thrown on' in the chorus very soon after joining the company in spite of the fact that I hardly knew the words, much less the moves, of any of the operas. I was so busy learning and rehearsing Peter's roles that any thought of memorising chorus parts just didn't come into it. So there I was among the baritones in *The Mikado,* 'goldfishing' away, with my eye on my fellow noblemen and trying to keep up with the elaborate fan work that went on. I was just thinking I was getting the hang of it, and executing a complicated gesture when my fan fell to pieces – the spokes became detached and I was left brandishing a long piece of material and feeling ridiculous. My early days as a chorister were certainly hair-raising, but I gradually learned words and moves and really began to enjoy the work. Of course, there was always the apprehension at the back of my mind that I could at any time be called upon to go on for Peter, but he seemed to be a pretty healthy person, and that very seldom happened.

Space permitting, there was usually a 'small part' room for principal understudies who also played minor roles, and I remember sharing with Fred Sinden, George Cook and John Fryatt, amongst others. Sometimes John and I would stay in between shows on a matinee day and practise different make-ups – something I would recommend strongly to amateur performers – and one day, for fun, we tried making up for a horror movie. I piled six *Mikado* wigs on my head, one on top of the other, giving the effect of a monstrous head, then proceeded to apply a ghoulish make-up. Johnny Fryatt did the same, and we crept up to the wardrobe where Cynthia was doing some ironing and poked our heads round the door. This caused her to let out a terrified shriek at the sight of the awful apparition and drop the iron! Our horror make-up had obviously been a success.

There was always plenty of fun to be had in the dressing room – keeping your sense of humour on a long tour is absolutely essential. At one theatre I happened to be sitting next to Jack Habbick, a baritone from the Glasgow area, and we became good friends. Jack always wore rubber heels on his shoes; they were round, and had one screw in the centre to hold the heel in place, so that you could turn it round as it wore down. He had lost one of these and went to buy a replacement, but as they were always sold in pairs he was left with a spare one, and we began to play games with it. I printed 'yes' on one side and 'no' on the other, and we spun it round and asked it ridiculous questions. Very silly, I suppose, but it became the centre of attention in the dressing room, and we got a lot of laughs out of it. At the end of the week as we were packing to move on to the next theatre, Jack handed me the heel. 'You can have this, John,' he said. 'I don't want the thing!' I replied, 'I never want to see it again as long as I live.'

The following week I was in a dressing room far away from Jack, but when I unlocked my case, there, wrapped in my make-up towel, was the heel. I never figured out how he had managed to put it there. Thus began years of passing that heel between Jack and myself, without either of us referring to it again. Sometimes it was weeks before it turned up – maybe as much as a month or more, and the methods of getting it from one to the other became more and more outrageous. Occasionally the transfer of the heel occurred on stage, but never by me, for everyone in the company was in on the joke. Once I had it placed on the block in *Yeomen,* for Jack played the executioner, and spotted it when he brought his axe down at the most dramatic moment, when nobody must laugh.

I even arranged for a policeman to come to the stage door and ask for Mr Habbick. Jack rushed down, wondering what on earth he had done, and the constable handed over the heel, saying, 'I believe this belongs to you, sir.' One Christmas time it was baked into a mince pie and offered to Jack, who was told it was bad luck to refuse it, and he must eat it without speaking, for that meant a happy month. So he took the pie, and immediately sank his teeth into it. I was listening outside the door of course, smothering my giggles, and heard in that wonderful Glasgow accent, 'It's the bloody heel!' There were so many equally amusing adventures of that heel as it travelled between us, each more ingenious than the last, and even after I became a principal the joke continued.

In 1961 Jack was appointed stage manager, and for some reason or other we quarrelled. I tried several times to patch it up with him, but he wouldn't have it, stubborn Scotsman that he was, so the heel was forgotten. I suspect that the new job turned out to be too much for him, for he seemed to become a different person, and stupidly we never spoke to each other again. When he left the company I lost track of the heel completely, and didn't even know who finally possessed it. Many years later I was clearing out the garden incinerator after burning some rubbish the previous day when I came upon an old Elastoplast tin, much charred by the fire. I managed to open it, and to my astonishment I found the heel – black and shrivelled – but still recognisable. At once I decided that it must go back to Jack somehow, and surely that would mend the rift between us. But, sadly, I found out that Jack had died – and on the very day the heel was burning. I gave it an honorable burial in the garden of my home in London, and I am quite sure that he has it once more and is most probably waiting for the day when he can return it – by 'angel post,' I hope.

My first American tour with the D'Oyly Carte with John Fryatt, Alice, Lorna and Cynthia.

In June 1955, after four years of touring, interspersed with London seasons, the company was to make an extensive coast-to-coast North American tour. I had mixed feelings about this, for it was a long time to be away from home, but it was undoubtedly an exciting prospect. I was to realise on subsequent American tours that this first one, when I was only a chorister and understudy, was the most enjoyable of all. I would always go over the opera to be played the next night just in case I had to go on for Peter, but that was all. I was free to go sightseeing, stay up late at parties and generally have a good time, whereas in the future, although I did not know it at the time, this sort of thing would not be possible. Peter was in every show, as were Joyce Wright and Ann Drummond Grant, whereas most of the others had free evenings when they were able to relax and enjoy themselves.

We were to sail to New York on the Queen Mary – that was exciting in itself, and after a farewell cocktail party at the Savoy we set off to Southampton to embark on the great ship. The first shock was that we could not even get a cup of tea or coffee, as it appeared that there was trouble among the catering staff. After an uneasy night on board we did at least get some breakfast, and made our way up on deck, thinking to wave goodbye to England. Then came the Captain's announcement – the ship would not sail. Apparently all the staff had walked off during the night, and we were soon to follow suit, trunks, cases and all, back to the Savoy. The management had held emergency meetings to determine how to get to get us all over to the States, and not just the acting members, but scenery, costumes and props, as well – everything must arrive in time. Mr Lloyd told us that we were to fly over by Stratocruiser. I did not wish to know about that, as I had never flown before – I don't believe any of us had, and I was very apprehensive. We all had to reduce our luggage to the obligatory forty-four pounds, and the problem of scaling down a great cabin trunk to a moderately-sized suitcase was monumental. But it had to be done, and at last the new case was packed to the exact weight, and the trunk sent home. It was a very dull day when we arrived at the airport, and at last we boarded, and I found myself in a seat next to Alan Styler. 'Oh, Alan,' I confessed, 'I'm not very mad about this.' 'Don't worry, John,' he said, pointing to the illuminated sign, 'Just fasten your seat belt and repeat after me: 'Our Father, which art in heaven . . . .' You may imagine, that was very reassuring! I have flown so many times since then; the USA, Canada, Australia, Italy, Denmark, but never once without Alan in my thoughts as I fasten that safety belt before take-off.

When we were safely airborne and had climbed through the clouds into the bright sunlight the captain announced his regret at not having had time to seat us as we would have preferred, and that we could now change places as we wished. Nobody seemed to be where they wanted to be, and everyone stood up immediately and milled about, except myself, who shouted out, 'Sit down for heaven's sake!' I thought they would overturn the plane – well, I did say it was my first flight.

After an overnight stop in New York, the tour took us to Central City, a unique venue, with a delightful little opera house. It was nearly two miles above sea level, up in the Rockies, and once the richest square mile on earth, so it was said. The gold rush days were at their height when Gilbert and Sullivan were writing the operas, and maybe for that reason we seemed to fit perfectly into the theatre and community there. We were the first British company ever to visit Central City and scored an instant success, both with the audiences and the local people, who took us immediately to their hearts. What a fascinating place it was, with its boardwalks, honky-tonk bars, Indian souvenir shops and the derelict goldmines which surrounded the small town. I suppose there were about three hundred inhabitants, and most of our audience came from Denver, forty miles away. We befriended Jim, the Sheriff, a real cowboy, complete with Stetson and guns on the hip. We were there for six weeks, and by the time we left everyone was involved with the friends and families who had adopted them. I shall never forget our departure. The buses which were to take us to Denver were to arrive at about 5 am, and nobody went to bed that last night. Central City was alive with activity – all our friends had gathered, supplying us with coffee, flowers and tears, and as we finally drove away Jim the Sheriff fired two shots into the air from the guns he had assured us had never been fired before. There were not many dry eyes on the buses as we left those wonderful people.

The rest of the tour took us to large cities such as San Francisco, Los Angeles, Chicago and New York, and up the east coast to Toronto and Montreal. It was all very exciting, but it is Central City that remains in my memory. Thirteen years later I returned as a principal, to find it just the same, and when I visited it again after I left the D'Oyly Carte and was directing at the University of Colorado at Boulder, I found it still held the same magic for me.

Our long American tour finished at the end of January 1956, and it was home to England, a welcome break, then back on the road again. Old friends left the company, including Cynthia in 1957, and new people joined, to become part of the D'Oyly Carte family. I continued with chorus work, my small parts and the occasional opportunity of playing one of Peter's roles, which happened so rarely that each time felt like a first performance. Goddie, Bruce Worsley (the company manager) and one or two others suggested to me that I should ask the management for one show a week possibly a matinee – so that I could become more accustomed to playing the roles. I was reluctant to do anything like this, but in the end I was persuaded, and wrote proposing this, but was refused. Was it perhaps time for me to leave and do other things, I wondered? But I stayed, and when the time came for contracts to be discussed in May 1959, I was asked to meet Mr Lloyd at the Randolph Hotel in Oxford, where we were currently playing at the New Theatre. All the others seemed to be discussing their contracts in the theatre, and I wondered why I alone should be summoned to an interview in a posh hotel.

I duly presented myself at the Randolph at the appointed hour and was greeted by Freddie Lloyd. 'Mr Pratt is leaving the company,' he announced. 'We would like you to take over his roles.' The news of Peter's imminent departure came as a complete shock. No rumours regarding such an event had circulated in the company. This, then, was what all my years of rehearsals and trial performances had been leading up to. So – 'Very well, Mr. Lloyd' I said.

CHAPTER 8

'Does your new employment please ye?'

('The Gondoliers)

After agreeing to take over the roles from Peter, I walked back to the theatre in a daze. What else could I have done? I suppose in an odd sort of way I considered it to be my duty – after all, I had been meticulously coached in the parts for nearly eight years, so maybe I had an obligation to take over now that I had been called upon to do so. As I turned the corner to the stage door I saw Peter standing there, puffing on his pipe. 'Have they told you?' he said. 'Yes,' I replied. 'Peter – are you sure you know what you're doing?' 'Oh, yes,' he said, 'I'm going.' I could not leave it like this. 'Let's get this straight, Peter,' I said, 'I never wanted these parts – I've always been perfectly happy as I am.' He made no comment, but continued to puff on his pipe. Then – 'I'm going,' he said – and go he did.

So it was in Oxford that I started my long career as principal comedian of the D'Oyly Carte Opera Company, and I set to work at once to win over the audiences who had been loyal followers of Peter Pratt for the past eight years. That was not an easy thing to do. I particularly remember two young men who regularly sat on the front row; they were great admirers of Peter, and hated it when I first took over. If I was on stage and getting laughs they refused to look at me, gazing round the audience as if to say,

'Whatever are you laughing at?' and rolling their eyes to the ceiling express their disgust that it was John Reed and not Peter Pratt on that stage. It was actually not all that long before they got over their disappointment, and I was accepted by them, but they were not accepted by me. In my vulnerable state at just having taken over the roles I had been deeply distressed by their insulting behaviour, and when they appeared at a reception I was attending I did not hesitate to tell them so in no uncertain terms. I don't remember seeing them in the front row any more. Sorry, Miss Carte, I thought, for the loss of two of your audience – but surely the sort we could do without.

It soon dawned on me that I was free to make all those wonderful characters my own, and no longer to be a carbon copy of my predecessor. So immersed was I in each character that on making an exit I would look back and almost expect Ko-Ko or Robin or Jack Point still to be standing on stage while John Reed returned to the dressing room. And although I was very nervous before every performance, still am in fact – when I got on to the stage the character would take over, and nerves would be forgotten. This doesn't happen so easily with Major General Stanley in *The Pirates of Penzance,* for the first thing he is confronted with is that tongue-twister of a song, and if you stumble or 'fluff' the words in that, it's almost impossible to redeem yourself completely during the rest of the opera. I know it's not considered to be a good thing to keep going over words in the wings just before you make an entrance, especially when it's a familiar number, but I never failed to do this where the Major General was concerned. That particular song consists of a lot of disconnected things following one another at breakneck speed, and it's difficult to think of a formula which unites them in the correct order. Whereas the Nightmare Song in *Iolanthe,* which I sang for my audition, does follow through nicely. There's continuity there, and you're telling a story. Having said that, there was an occasion much later on when I reached the line, 'And you dream you are crossing the channel and tossing about in a steamer from Harwich' – well, I just couldn't get off that steamer! The next word should have been 'which' but do you think I could find it? After what seemed ages, I did, and was away safely to the end of the number – the delay probably only lasted a second or two, but to me it seemed like a lifetime.

Feeling nervous was not just reserved for big gala nights or performances when royalty or when some important person was in front. I felt just the same at a matinee in Morecambe as for a first night in New York – every audience deserves the best you can give. There are no short cuts, no giving less than your best at any time. If you think otherwise, amateur or professional, then I fear the stage is not for you.

Just as I was taking over the principal roles, a new recording *of HMS Pinafore* was announced, and I found that I was recording Sir Joseph before I had actually played him on stage in my new capacity. This seemed a typically topsy-turvy thing to do.

Number one dressing room proved at first to be rather a lonely place after the camaraderie of the small parts room, to which I had long been accustomed. I was proud of my years in the chorus – indeed I considered it the very best way to become familiar with the operas and aware of all the somewhat quaint traditions of the D'Oyly Carte. I did not wish to become a different person now that I had achieved my new status, but I did notice that the attitude towards me of some of my former colleagues in the chorus had undergone a subtle change. This was not my doing, but theirs. Previously, the dressing room now allocated to me had been a 'no-go' area, very few people had ventured into the inner sanctum to disturb the previous incumbent before, during or after the show. I was, I supposed, expected to slip into the way of my predecessor, but this was contrary to my nature and visitors were always welcome. Sometimes, when space backstage was limited. I would share with Kenneth Sandford, which made things a little more convivial, though I could have done without the tenor arias with which he regularly warmed up! Was there a frustrated Pavarotti lurking within that baritone exterior, I sometimes wondered?

As I became more at ease with the roles I began to mould them to fit my own personality. I think of them as acting parts more than anything, and most call for a certain amount of dancing – especially where the encores are concerned. Peter Pratt was a bass, whereas I – well let's just say I had a natural singing voice. When I began to learn the roles Bill Cox-Ife, who was chorus master and assistant conductor said to me, 'John, don't have any more singing lessons,' (I hadn't had any, to be honest!) 'Your voice is placed just right for these parts.' That was good enough for me. And I've always danced, so made the most of every opportunity to do so. In addition to these possible attributes, I was the right size and fitted the costumes – probably the most essential qualification of all!

I had long ago become used to the idea that every word of Gilbert's was sacred, and no variation of text or changing of a single word, however insignificant would be tolerated. When I was new to the company this was a revelation, for in weekly rep, with all those lines to be learned in such a short time, you got the gist of each speech, gave the correct cue, and that was quite acceptable. I had certainly never seen members of the audience sitting there with libretto or score, checking the words and music throughout the show. In fact, after one of my first understudy performances I was waylaid by a teenage girl at the stage door with, 'Very good tonight, only one mistake: you said 'and' instead of 'but' when,' – I waited to hear no more. It's incredible, but quite true, I assure you. I remember hearing of an amateur performance of *Patience* in Dublin, where there were a number of nuns in the audience, some of whom were sitting in the front row with scores on their laps, following the opera word for word. It seemed they were to produce the show for some church group or other. The chap who was playing Bunthorne, seeing what was going on, looked down between verses of his song and said loudly, 'Is that roight Sister?' I don't know what happened next!

Kenneth Sandford, who of course was playing all the baritone roles at that time (Pooh-Bah, Grosvenor, Don Alhambra etc) and I worked very well together. He was so right for those parts, and always worked hard at them. As we grew more used to playing together, I could look into his eyes and tell exactly what he was thinking, what mood he was in, and how to react. His Dr Daly was superb.

With Ken Sandford in *The Gondoliers*.

Ann Drummond Grant, wife of Isidore Godfrey, who played all the principal contralto roles, sadly died in September 1959, so I had little chance to work with her. Alice Hynd temporarily took over, then the following season Gillian Knight, a slim young woman with a surprisingly deep voice, joined the company to play the parts on a permanent basis. She had to wear a considerable amount of padding to look right for her roles, and I used at first to help her with her make-up, for WS Gilbert did not often require beauty in his contralto characters – rather the reverse! Apart from the Fairy Queen and to a lesser degree the Duchess of Plaza-Toro, Gillian was obliged to don quite a heavy character make-up for her roles, both for the purpose of ageing and looking less attractive. We started playing our new roles at more or less the same time, and we formed a very good working relationship, becoming good friends as well, as we are to this day. One night during *The Gondoliers* we were waiting to make our entrance as the Duke and Duchess of Plaza-Toro, and I said jokingly, 'Come on, you old bag, let's get on stage!' Whereupon Gillian replied, 'All right, you gas bag,' for I always talked too much – still do. Before we knew it, everyone wanted to be a bag, and people were asking, 'Can we join the Bag Family?' Anne Sessions became the 'Jewel Bag', as she always wore a lot of costume jewellery; Cis Blain, our wardrobe mistress, was inevitably the 'Laundry Bag', and one of the baritones became known as the 'Tool Bag' . . . . . .

As I settled into the roles I began to attract a number of fans, as did, I'm sure, Peter, Martyn Green and all the other principal comedians in their time. Most were delightful people, but one or two became an awful nuisance, and would follow me home from the theatre to find out where I lived. I did not like this at all, and would try to give them the slip by turning suddenly down a side street, but often in vain. Even when I lived in a quiet little mews tucked right away from the busy streets they would follow me somehow, find out where I lived, and I would discover a note stuck behind the windscreen wiper of my car the following morning. I suppose it was a kind of game as far as they were concerned, and maybe I made it worse by trying to avoid them. I saw one well-known fan of the company standing in the mews one morning at ten o'clock, just gazing at my house. I simply couldn't understand it at all. I wanted to leave my characters in the theatre where they belonged, and return to my private life as John Reed.

I acquired a fan soon after I took over, who was a bus conductress, later becoming a driver, and she would sit in the audience in her uniform and wait at the stage door after the performance. She used to drive a van, and followed the company all round the country – Liverpool, Bournemouth, Manchester – you name it – she was there. When she ever went to work, goodness knows. I had a white MG at the time, of which I was very fond, and lo and behold – she painted her van white too – but not content with that, she painted my characters all round the van, and they were so obviously *me*. It was very flattering, but most embarrassing to have this van following me from whatever venue the company had been playing back to London after the show every Saturday night. This went on for a long time, and I remember particularly well one occasion in Hull. After two performances of *The Mikado* I jumped into my car to drive all the way back to London for the weekend, and after negotiating the city centre and approach roads I finally reached the A1. And there it was, the Van, moving very slowly, and obviously waiting for me. It was the only road I could possibly take – and she knew it. To say I was irritated would be putting it mildly, so I put my foot down and sped past. A few miles farther on I ran into thick fog, and inevitably slowed down. I hate driving in fog at the best of times, and was very tired, which made matters worse. Shortly after that the van passed me, and waved me down. She got out, came to me and said, "John, you must be very tired. May I lead you back to London?" This she did – and how grateful I was for those reassuring rear lights ahead of me on that foggy night. Twice she pulled off the Al, asking if I'd like coffee. The second time I closed my eyes and maybe nodded off for a moment or two. I awoke to find her and her friend walking quietly round the car to see if I was awake. How often does one find such devotion? At that moment I realised what I meant to them, and my whole attitude changed. How lucky I was to have fans like that – I would never turn them away again. So, thank you, little bus driver – you taught me such a lesson, and let me say now how much I appreciate those years of devotion. It might have been embarrassing to start with, but I hadn't realised that – especially where the D'Oyly Carte was concerned – that sort of thing went with the job.

CHAPTER 9

'Professional licence, if carried too far. . . .' *(Iolanthe)*

A good relationship with the conductor is very important, and I always found that working under Goddie's baton was both comfortable and pleasant. His tempi were just right for everything I had to do, which was only to be expected, for the young Isidore Godfrey had joined the D'Oyly Carte in 1926 as assistant musical director to Harry Norris. In May 1929 he took over on the podium, and there he remained until 1968 – an amazing forty-two years.

The only times we had any differences of opinion were when I introduced pieces of business of which he did not approve. I was always extremely careful that anything new did not interfere with the integrity of the opera in any way, but occurred either in encores, of which more later, or at some other suitable point.

For instance, in the finale of *Iolanthe,* when the Fairy Queen decreed that everyone was henceforth a fairy, wings sprang from the shoulders of all the peers, including the Lord Chancellor. These were cunningly concealed, folded flat, and released by the discreet removal of a restraining pin by the person nearest to you. It always got a laugh as they were revealed, and one day I thought, why don't I make mine flap? The audience would love that. And after all, it would be quite an appropriate thing to do, seeing we were just about to take off for Fairyland. The wings were kept apart at the right angle by a small chain, so I attached some black tape to the centre of that, opened a seam in my costume, brought the tape through, round to the front and fixed the end to a button on my waistcoat. All I had to do was to jerk the tape, and the wings flapped most convincingly. When Goddie witnessed this for the first time, he was furious, refused to look at me, and conducted the rest of the show with his head down, sulking. But as for the audience – well, they loved it, and that's what mattered to me. I kept it in, but Goddie always hated it. The funny thing is, he invited me out one night after *Iolanthe* for drinks with some friends of his, and the first thing one of the ladies said was, 'Oh, John, I do love the way you flap your wings in the finale – it's so funny!' I laughed. 'Goddie hates it,' I said, but he just grunted and made no reply. It was one of the few points on which we agreed to differ.

I always thought it rather hard on Goddie when celebrity guest conductors were invited to do certain first nights and special occasions at the Savoy. After all, he'd done all the hard work on the tour, and it didn't seem fair that he should have to take a back seat at important times like that. I remember when Sir Malcolm Sargent was to conduct a performance of *The Gondoliers,* the ducal party – Gillian Knight (Duchess), Jennifer Toye (Casilda), Philip Potter (Luiz) and myself were called to rehearse our ensemble numbers at his flat at 9, Royal Albert Hall Mansions. I was quite nervous at the thought of working with this famous conductor. He sat down at one of his two grand pianos and played the introduction to the number, 'from the sunny Spanish shore' and as I opened my mouth to sing he stopped abruptly. 'I'll never forget Henry Lytton doing this' – he said – 'He was so marvellous.' Then he repeated the intro and I prepared to start the number. Again he paused, laughing, leaving me with my mouth open. 'Oh, I remember Henry Lytton did so-and-so just here,' Yet again the introduction was played, and once more Sargent stopped. 'I'll never forget Henry Lytton as he' – I could stand no more. 'Look here, Sir Malcolm', I said, 'Henry Lytton's dead and gone! You've got *me,* now.' After that, the rehearsal continued without further reminiscences, and when we finished, he said, 'Thank you, everyone, that's all. John, would you stay for a few minutes?' Now I'm going to get told off, I thought, but when the others had gone, Sir Malcolm simply said, 'Sit down, John – can you stay for some sherry?' And we sat and chatted about this and that – nothing about Henry Lytton at all!

Another encounter with Sir Malcolm occurred at an *Iolanthe* rehearsal in the theatre. I was up on stage, and started the Nightmare Song, and I'd only sung a few lines when he stopped and addressed the orchestra. 'You're playing a B flat there, violins – it should be a B natural,' or some such thing. Then he pointed at me and we resumed. A few lines later he stopped again to point out something to the orchestra, then we went on. This happened a few times, and I finally rebelled. 'Just a minute, Sir Malcolm,' I said, 'Are you going to stop any more? Because if you are, you'll have to come up here and sing it yourself. This is a song with continuity, and I've got to sing it tonight. I can't work like this – it's quite impossible.' He mumbled a bit, but gave way and we rehearsed as I wanted. I don't often take a stand like that, but I can if I have to.

I had number one dressing room at the Savoy – it was nearest the stage, and convenient for my many comings and goings. Imagine my surprise when I went in after the interval to find Sir Malcolm ensconced there being served refreshments by a waiter from the hotel. 'Oh, don't go,' I said with heavy irony, which almost certainly passed unnoticed, 'I don't mind you being here.' Of course, he had his own dressing room – it was probably not as nice as mine, and up a few stairs, so he chose my room in preference. Ah well, I thought, it was only for a couple of performances.

Another memory of Sir Malcolm and *The Gondoliers* concerns the Cachucha – the exuberant dance in Act II. I had spent some time on it with the chorus, trying to make it more exciting, introducing a few new steps and generally giving it a face-lift. I was standing in the stalls at the Savoy with Freddie Lloyd during an orchestral rehearsal in order to watch it, and was horrified at the slow tempo – the chorus couldn't dance to it, some were trying, and others had given up altogether. Freddie whispered to me, 'It's too slow, isn't it?' 'Yes,' I replied, 'It certainly is.' 'Tell him,' said Freddie. 'Why don't *you?*' I suggested, but he didn't, so I turned to Sir Malcolm and said, 'It's too slow.' 'What?' he said crossly, turning round, amazed that anyone should criticise his tempo. He called up to the chorus, '*Is* it too slow?' 'Yes!' they answered unanimously, by which time I was through the pass door and up on the stage, stomping through the steps of the Cachucha to show him the exact tempo required. I must say he did comply, and afterwards had the grace to say to me, 'I'm sorry – I didn't realise you were in charge of the dance.'

I wasn't the only D'Oyly Carte comedian to have an altercation with Sir Malcolm by any means, though I was unaware of it at the time. Sir Henry Lytton, when playing King Gama in *Princess Ida* was furious at the brisk tempo employed by the then Dr Sargent for his opening number, and was heard to say as he came off stage, 'I'm supposed to be lame. I walk with a stick. An old crock can't walk that fast. The man's an idiot. He just *won't* learn.' On another occasion at the same point in the opera Lytton ignored Sargent's introductory tempo, came right down to the footlights and sang the number through at his own slower speed, emphasising the beat by tapping his stick on the stage, to no avail. The orchestra finished two bars ahead, as Sargent refused to adjust to Lytton's tempo. It seems that the audience thought it was all part of the act, and laughed uproariously.

Another anecdote about Dr Malcolm Sargent's intransigence occurs early in Martyn Green's career, before he took over the principal roles from Sir Henry Lytton. He was playing Antonio in *The Gondoliers,* a small part with a lively song at the beginning of Act I which calls for some quick little dance steps. The music was too slow, Martyn could neither sing nor dance it at that speed, so he stopped altogether. Sargent asked what was the matter, and when Martyn explained, replied, 'You know nothing about it. That is the tempo I am setting, and that is the tempo at which it will be taken.'

Martyn pointed out that it was impossible to dance it at that speed, as there was a law of gravity that said when you went up you had to come down, and that set its own tempo. Sargent was annoyed and still refused to change anything. However, later in the day some sort of compromise was eventually reached, albeit rather grudgingly.

After all these rather downbeat stories about Sir Malcolm, I have to say that when he was conducting, not a performance went by without him popping his head round the door at the fall of curtain to say, 'Well done!' 'A good show tonight,' or something of that sort. Nobody else had ever done that, and it meant a lot to me.

The prospect of singing some G&S at the Scottish Proms under the baton of Charles Mackerras (soon to be *Sir* Charles) made me feel rather nervous. I knew him to be a great Gilbert and Sullivan afficionado, and like countless others I admired his brilliant arrangement of Sullivan's music for the charming *Pineapple Poll* ballet. I had heard on the '*Desert Island Discs*' radio programme that he and his family, back in Australia, were such G&S fans that they had occasionally been known to converse entirely in Gilbert's words and lyrics – I must say that I have never gone to those lengths!

Charles Mackerras was the exact opposite of Sir Malcolm Sargent. At the orchestral rehearsal I was singing one of my numbers when he tapped his stand and brought it to a halt. Here we go again, I thought. Nothing of the sort. He addressed the musicians, saying, 'Don't rush it, ladies and gentlemen, can't you hear he wants to take it a little slower? Allow him to then, now, let's start again.' There was no question of imposing *his* tempo it was *mine* that was important. That really gave an enormous boost to my confidence – it seemed that after all those years I had some authority to perform a number in the way I wanted, and not necessarily the way it had always been done. To learn that from an internationally renowned conductor like Mackerras was invaluable to me.

To celebrate the centenary of *Trial by Jury* in 1975 the company played for two weeks at the Savoy, and Goddie made a return appearance to conduct *HMS Pinafore*. Charles Mackerras was invited to conduct *The Pirates of Penzance* and *The Mikado,* and it was a great pleasure to work with him again.

On May 2nd 1977 I received a letter from 10 Downing Street informing me that I was to be considered for an OBE, and confirmation of this arrived on October 12th. This news was very exciting, and I asked my two sisters, Betty and Anne, if they would like to attend the Investiture. Of course, they were absolutely thrilled, and new outfits were discussed and bought. It was a great adventure for all three of us to drive through the great gates into the forecourt of Buckingham Palace. I had met the Queen many times before, but my sisters had never seen her in person, so all in all it was a great day for them. I was doubly pleased to see that Charles Mackerras, who had previously been awarded an OBE, was to receive a knighthood on that very same day.

John Reed with his two sisters after receiving his OBE

CHAPTER 10

'In Friendship's Name' *(Iolanthe)*

I really can't remember when I first met Nick, nor can he. It seems we've always known each other. It might have been at a party – there were so many during the D'Oyly Carte's London seasons. We ran into each other a few times after that and got chatting about things in general. I told him how my flat had recently been burgled and I was worried about going on tour. 'Where do you live?' Nick asked. 'North London,' I replied. 'Do you know Tufnell Park Road, it's just off Holloway Road, not very far from the tube.' 'Oh, yes,' he replied, 'I often pass that way, I'm always on the road to somewhere or other.'

Nick was works manager of an engineering firm in south east London, and had a flat in Blackheath, and his job involved a lot of travelling. The outcome of our conversation was that he offered to look in frequently to check that everything was all right in the flat while I was away. I felt very much relieved at this, for although I had excellent neighbours, they were out at work all day. I introduced Nick to Marie and David, who lived next door, gave him a key, and all was arranged. The burglary had upset me, not because my tape recorder and television had been stolen – these were easily replaceable – but because all the tapes of my mother's voice had also gone. But I can always hear her voice in my head – that's better than any tapes.

I no longer had a home in Darlington, for everything had been sold up on my mother's death, so I had decided that a base in London would be my best option. Most of the company's time was spent on tour, but any lengthy seasons were always in London, so at least I would be able to settle down then, if only for a little while. I set out on tour feeling much easier in my mind, with someone to keep an eye on the flat. Nick told me he called in once and saw some strange shoots poking out beneath a cupboard – I'd left some potatoes there, and they'd sprouted. They'd probably have been halfway across the kitchen floor by the time I was home again if he hadn't called in and cleared them up!

A tour of the USA and Canada was announced in 1962. The company was to open in Pasadena on the 13th August and we were to be away until January 1963, about five months in all. Unlike most of the others, I was not particularly thrilled about this. I suppose I am a home bird at heart, though that seems an extraordinary thing to say, seeing that I have spent most of my life on tour.

The next time I saw Nick he told me that the lease on his flat in Blackheath would be up shortly, and he was house hunting. An idea occurred to me. 'Look here. Nick', I said, 'This is a two-bedroomed flat with lots of room and it's empty most of the time. I'm off to America soon for five months – why don't you move in – at least for the time being?' After some discussion this was agreed on, and I was able to leave for the tour of the States with my mind at rest. When I returned, we would talk things over again.

The North American tour of 1962 was my first as a principal, and very different from that of 1955-56, when as a chorister I was able to relax, go to parties and do a lot of sight-seeing. Not this time. I was on for every performance and it was absolutely necessary to rest and conserve all my energy for the show each night, and matinees as well, of course. And what a tour that was – some of the visits were so brief – two days in Portland, Calgary and Minneapolis, three in Vancouver and Edmonton, and a one night stand in

Saskatoon – such a lot of travelling. It was a relief to spend two weeks in some of the larger cities, and four in New York – at least we were able to unpack. Any spare time I had was taken up by television and radio interviews, but I felt I was establishing myself in the roles with American audiences.

There was a time in Chicago that I remember very well indeed. We had done a very good *Mikado* the previous night, with all the usual encores vociferously demanded, and a wonderful reception at the final curtain. But the following day there was a really terrible review in one of the papers. No member of the cast was any good at all, and the whole show was pretty well written off. Everyone was absolutely dejected when they read it. The author of this damning report was a woman called Claudia Cassidy.

We moved on to the next city with considerable relief and after a successful first night four of the principals, including myself, were to be interviewed in the foyer of the theatre. Tom Round was already there when I arrived, and we were waiting for Gillian Knight and Jennifer Toye to join us. I was handed a microphone, and the interviewer mentioned something about a critic. That was like a red rag to a bull. 'Don't mention critics to me!' I said, 'Take that Claudia Cassidy from Chicago, for one – she must be as old as God, anyway.' Because everyone laughed I continued, 'And I bet she's got a face like the back of a bus!' The girls arrived just then and the interview began, or so I thought. I was horrified to discover later that everything had gone out on air. Heaven help me, I thought, she'll slaughter me next time we play Chicago, and really she hadn't been so bad about me as the others. However, a few years later when we visited Chicago again, I couldn't put a foot wrong for her. Oh, yes, Claudia, I thought – two can play at that game, my girl.

When at last the American tour ended it was good to get home to my flat and find it warm, bright and welcoming, with food in the fridge and everything ready for my return. Nick stayed on – we found sharing the flat worked very well – and I was off on tour again in a couple of weeks. Nick had become weary of all the constant travelling associated with his work and decided to give in his notice and look around for something else. While doing this he went to the Savoy Theatre, of all places, to work temporarily as a dresser. The play currently running there was *The Secretary Bird,* and he found himself looking after that much-loved actor, John Gregson. They got on extremely well – John G called Nick 'the best dressed dresser in the West End', and frequently asked to borrow his tie if he was suddenly asked out after the show, for he certainly never wore one to the theatre himself. Now and then he would present Nick with a bottle or two of his favourite Italian wine; he was a charming and delightful man. During this time the chief electrician, Simon Leverton, affectionately known as 'Simmie' approached Nick to ask if he would be interested in learning the switchboard with the view of becoming assistant electrician at the Savoy. 'That's right up my street,' replied Nick accepting the offer with enthusiasm. He spent several happy years working with Simmie, both in the theatre, and going on after the show to light the cabaret at the Savoy Hotel. It was hard work, for it meant doing a morning shift as well, setting up for the evening, but Nick enjoyed it and liked working with Simmie, so he didn't mind.

I remember one amusing incident which occurred while I was still living at Tufnell Park. I'd walked down to the tube station, musing on how I might do something different in the encores to the 'Bell' trio in *Pinafore* that night. The 'Twist' was all the rage just then, so I thought, I'll put that in. I got into the lift at the station – it was one of those big old-fashioned ones, with sliding iron gates at each end, and it was empty. My mind was focussed on the Twist, and being all alone, I went into an energetic routine as the lift descended. I was completely carried away, and hardly noticed when the lift stopped at platform level. Imagine my embarrassment when I saw crowds of people all staring in at me with great interest. The gates opened and, shame-faced I made my exit to a great round of applause! Well, that seems to work, I decided – I'll put it in tonight!

Much as we loved the flat, the day came when we felt it was time to make a move to somewhere slightly larger. Having explored several areas we found a delightful mews house in a secluded position a mere stone's throw from Notting Hill Gate. I think what clinched matters for us was that the house was in Rede Place! Although the name was spelt differently from mine, we thought that 'John Reed of Rede Place' sounded rather good. We bought everything new for the little house, and it looked really lovely. We spent eight years there and loved it.

I remember calling in to see Cynthia one day when I was passing that way. She lived with her clarinettist husband, Anthony Jennings, in Mount Pleasant Road, Brondesbury Park. It was a lovely tree-lined road, and the houses, built in the late twenties to thirties, were large, with extensive gardens. 'I think I'd like to live here,' I said. 'Well, why don't you?' she answered, 'There's one for sale across the road.' No sooner said than done. The estate agent was only just round the corner, so I arranged an immediate viewing. As soon as I got into the house, I knew. 'I want it!' I said. Of course, I shouldn't have said anything at all in front of the vendor – I should have been non-committal, gone back to the agent and made a lowish offer. But that's not my way. Needless to say, Nick was as enthusiastic as I, and in due course we moved in. It was then that we were able to have a dog – our beautiful Boxer, Sheba.

We went to choose a dog at a kennels down in Sussex, and looked at all the available puppies in their enclosures. They came yapping excitedly to us – all except one, a Boxer pup who sat at the back of her pen and just looked at us with great soulful eyes. We were lost.

Although we'd had the notion of getting a Bedlington terrier, that idea vanished as soon as we saw Sheba. She turned out to be the most wonderful companion, toured with me and accompanied me to the theatre. I shall never forget her.

One day, when I was still living in Tufnell Park, Miss Carte invited me to a meal at the Savoy. We were to discuss, of all things, a new hat for Bunthorne. 'What sort of hat do you think you should have, Mr Reed?' she asked. I looked at her – she was wearing a floppy velvet beret. 'As a matter of fact, Miss Carte,' I said, 'I'd like a hat rather like the one you're wearing. You know, a beret like artists wear.' And shortly afterwards I got exactly the hat I had described.

I wrote to Miss Carte to thank her for entertaining me, and said I'd like to return the compliment – would she come for dinner one Sunday? Wanting to make it sound informal I added a PS: 'by the way – I make smashing chocolate éclairs.' She replied, saying she'd like to come very much, adding 'I love chocolate éclairs.' A date was arranged, and Miss Carte arrived in a large limousine, with some gorgeous flowers. I took her coat in our small hall, noting how beautiful it was. 'What a lovely coat,' I remarked, 'What is it?' She gave an enigmatic little smile, and answered, 'Fur.' Of course, I knew that it was something exotic and no doubt fabulously expensive – Russian mink perhaps. I showed her into the lounge and proceeded to hang that priceless coat in our broom cupboard! I wonder what she would have thought if she'd known it was hanging up among all our brushes and mops and hoover!

That was the beginning of many visits from Miss Carte – she really seemed to relax when she was away from her apartment at the hotel, and she must have enjoyed herself or she wouldn't have come again. She invariably arrived in a chauffeur-driven car, with gorgeous flowers or a plant for us, and we drove her back to the

Savoy at the end of the evening. We chatted about all manner of things, but never about company matters, and she always addressed me as 'Mr Reed' though she called Nick 'Nicholas'. I was talking about my family one evening, and I asked her where her mother lived, 'Oh,' replied Miss Carte vaguely, 'You just go down to the Bahamas and turn left.' I thought that remark absolutely typical of her.

She also visited us at the mews house, and at Mount Pleasant Road, where, sinking down on to a comfortable sofa, she'd kick off her shoes and curl up with a glass of scotch and a cigarette. I felt awkward calling her 'Miss Carte' in my own home; I certainly couldn't possibly call her 'Bridget' so sometimes just called her 'dear'. She wasn't Dame Bridget at that time – perhaps that would have been easier. She seemed to enjoy my cooking, and remarked once, 'How lovely to have warm plates – I don't get that at the Savoy.' On one of her visits I suggested she pop upstairs to leave her coat, and she came down holding out a pair of mink ear muffs which she'd found on the bed. 'What are these?' she asked. 'They're ear muffs,' I said, 'I bought them in America. You can have them if you like.' So she went home in them that night – they matched her coat rather well, I thought. I liked Bridget D'Oyly Carte very much, and felt that she was a lonely woman, glad of a chance to relax in someone's ordinary comfortable home, far away from the formalities of the Savoy.

When the D'Oyly Carte presented a new production, such as the new *Gondoliers* or *The Sorcerer,* there would be a reception in the hotel, at which costume and set designs were displayed. Various business people were invited, usually including quite a number of Americans. I would see Dame Bridget's anguished face across the room, and she would make her way through the crowd to me. 'Oh, Mr Reed,' she'd say, 'Do come and talk to these Americans for me – you do it so much better than I do.' So I'd go and chat to them. I've never had any difficulty in talking to anyone – stopping me is another matter! But she, poor dear, was really painfully shy, and I believe her shyness was often mistaken for standoffishness. But I knew better.

At a reception at the Savoy with Dame Bridget

By this time Nick had risen to the position of assistant manager at the Savoy Theatre, a job he held for a number of years. Then one day we decided we were both a little tired of living in London, and as I was almost always on tour we thought it might be a good idea to move somewhere quite different, maybe the seaside. As soon as we mentioned the idea of moving, Cynthia and Tony said they would be interested in buying our house, which was bigger and had a nicer garden than theirs. Nick had always fancied the idea of running a small hotel, and we both liked Bournemouth very much, so went to have a look round.

Our first venture was Holly Tree House, which Nick ran very efficiently, and enjoyed the work. Before long, I was off with the company to Australia. I really did not want to do that tour, and had a long discussion with Freddie Lloyd on the subject, trying to find some way to get out of it. I was made to feel that I would be putting the whole project in jeopardy if I refused to go, so I was eventually persuaded to give in, much against my will. I left the company at the end of that tour.

I remember one morning shortly after my return to England, when Nick was busy with the guests' breakfasts, I decided to get in the car and see a bit of Bournemouth, for I had never had the leisure time to look around, and knew little of the town. I noticed a very nice hotel with a 'For Sale' board outside, and stopped to have a look at it. It was larger than Holly Tree House, obviously with more accommodation, and a large parking area in front. I drove home, thinking hard. 'What do you think, Nicky,' I said, 'I've just seen such a nice hotel for sale.' 'Oh, no!' he groaned, throwing up his hands in horror – but I persisted. 'It's called the Southernhay, and it's in such a good position, shall we go and see it?' Well, we did, and to cut a long story short, we bought it. There was much more room for our own quarters than at Holly Tree, and we soon settled in. It was hard work, but Nicky liked doing it, and was obviously good at it.

Some time later I called to see Cynthia, who now lived in our old house and she told me some disturbing news. 'Dame Bridget's very ill,' she said, 'apparently it hasn't been made public – I don't know why.' I was sorry to hear this, but didn't have any idea how serious her condition was. I was deeply shocked to read in the paper the following day that she had died at her home in Buckinghamshire. It was May 2nd 1985, six years after I had left the D'Oyly Carte. I hadn't been in touch for some time, and I regretted that very much. I would miss her.

CHAPTER 11

'That's how I'd play this part' – (*The Grand Duke*)

'The characters you play are all so varied – how do you go about playing a different one every night?'

That's a difficult question for me, but one I have been asked many times by G&S fans. I find the answer hard to put into words. When I'm directing I can show anyone how to do *anything*; writing down what I do is something quite different. However, I'll try. But when coaching an actor in these roles I would not expect him to play the character exactly as I do, but would encourage him to invest it with his own personality.

To start with the basics – you've got to *look* right, which brings us first to make-up. To keen amateur performers I would advise that you practise different character make-ups, and practise often. For instance, the Judge, the Lord Chancellor, Sir Joseph Porter and Major General Stanley need, according to the age of the actor playing them – an elderly make-up. The Judge and the Lord Chancellor, who spend most of their time indoors, require a pale base, but the Major General needs something rather healthier. After all, he's been on a lot of campaigns, probably in hot climates, and his brandy flask is almost certainly kept handy. For Sir Joseph, again rather pale – after all, he spent his youth in an office before going into Parliament, and has never been to sea, apart from the occasional visits he makes to ships of the 'Queen's Navee,' safely at anchor. All these gentlemen should have carefully-applied lines to age the actor who is playing them – unless he already has lines of his own, of course! Even then, these may need subtly enhancing, as stage lighting will lessen their impact. Age lines must always be applied in the *right* place – to find where this is, wrinkle up your face to see where lines will eventually materialise, (and believe me, they will!) then lightly mark them in, very slightly blurring them so that they don't look too hard and artificial.

The Judge, although a learned man, has an impish sense of humour, a twinkle in the eye, and a partiality for the ladies. This is first shown when he makes his entrance, waving to an attractive girl in the box, and the fact that he ends up with the Plaintiff confirms his susceptibility to feminine charm.

The Learned Judge,
Trial by Jury

The Lord Chancellor is of course also a legal character, entering in a most dignified way and deferred to by all the Peers. He is an elderly gentlemen and should show this in his stance and in the way he walks. He maintains dignity, with a few amusing touches, right through the opera until the trio 'If You Go In' with Tolloller and Mountararat in Act II. Then, and only then, he lets his hair down and shows a surprisingly nimble pair of legs, capering about in a most un-chancellor - like way which usually calls for several encores, each getting more lively and inventive. Now comes a very important point: he must immediately snap back into his former character as if all this frivolity had never happened. Prolonging the comedy will not work, in fact it will spoil it completely. And there is a very poignant moment at the end when Iolanthe reveals herself, and when the Lord Chancellor says, his voice breaking with emotion, 'Iolanthe – thou livest'. This must be handled with great sensitivity. The words are actually written to music, but I – and many others before me, no doubt – have found it more effective to speak them.

Now we come to Sir Joseph Porter, supremely elegant, beautifully groomed, and – let me make this important point – without a single crease in his immaculate white breeches, or a sign of a wrinkle in his white stockings. He must be impeccably turned out – nothing less will do. That is why, when he lets his hair down briefly in the 'Bell' trio in the second act, the contrast in his demeanour makes such an impact. Again, when the encores are over, he must immediately resume his dignity as if nothing untoward had happened. Any suspicion of such frivolity in subsequent scenes will destroy the characterisation. It is the impact of the totally unexpected which provokes the laughter.

Talking of encores, I regard them as a bit of fun between me and the audience. And they must all be different, leaving the audience agog to see what will happen next. Encores should never be done unless they're really called for, and the applause goes on for so long that it's impossible to proceed. To put in a pre-determined number of encores 'because they're always done,' is simply not on. The first two that we did after the 'Bell' trio were fairly routine – mainly dancing the Charleston and ringing all sorts of bells. One which got a lot of laughs was when I pushed an imaginary door bell, turned away, then the percussion player in the orchestra played a loud chime, which made me turn back in amazement. We had a lot of fun with this, and with all the other kinds of bells which evolved, different every time. More and more encores were demanded for the trio and I had to rack my brains for new ideas. I hid some flags on the ship at the back, produced them and signalled 'SOS' to the other ship painted on the backcloth at least – I hoped the audience guessed what I intended, as I didn't really know the code. It so happened that some of us were invited to a reception at the Admiralty one evening after a performance of *HMS Pinafore,* and we were introduced to the First Lord as we went in. 'Ah,' I said, 'You're just the gentleman I need to speak to. I want to know how to signal 'SOS' in semaphore.' He laughed, and replied, 'Don't ask *me* – 'I've no idea. You'd better speak to the Commander over there.' Now, why on earth did I imagine the First Lord of the Admiralty would know anything about naval matters? Gilbert knew exactly what he was writing about: 'Stick close to your desks and never go to sea, and you all may be Rulers of the Queen's Navee'. He certainly got it right. By the way, the Commander hadn't got a clue either.

After the semaphore, the audience demanded yet another encore. I hired a lifebelt and arranged for Ken Sandford to stand by with it in the wings. I had examined the set minutely so that I knew exactly where to make my new move. At the appropriate moment I went up to the back, nipped my nose with my fingers and jumped overboard. Consternation reigned – Goddie nearly fell off his podium and the orchestra were craning their necks to see what was going on. I reappeared wearing the lifebelt, pulled a large fish out of my jacket, (Nick and I had sat up till two am that morning to make it!) threw it into the orchestra and continued with the trio. The very last time of all I disappeared, then could be seen paddling to and fro in the sea at the back on an imaginary raft with a mast and sail made from a white shirt, wired to keep it rigid. I re-entered with mast and sail which resembled a banner, and as we finished singing, pointed to the words written on the shirt tail: THE END. As I made my exit one of the orchestra handed me back a large fishbone as if they'd eaten the fish for supper. The opera was at last able to continue.

Major General Stanley wasn't nearly as much fun, in fact it was a role I gave up after several years, wanting to have the occasional

Major General Stanley,
The Pirates of Penzance

night off. Eight performances a week is hard going, and I needed a little time to myself. The Major General is confronted with his rather daunting song as he makes his first entrance. As I've mentioned before, it's a list of completely unrelated items, which are very tricky to memorise. Linking words to moves can be a help; if you can think to yourself, 'I go stage right for 'I know our mythic history' and stage left for 'Mamelon and ravelin' it's possible to work out some sort of plan to help you with the order of words. Once the song is safely over you can relax and enjoy yourself, but the rest of the part is fairly unrewarding – or so it seems to me, though I'm sure there are many who enjoy playing it. One comment – never forget his soldierly bearing and incisive voice – this is a man who is used to giving orders. In the second act opening you can show a little of his softer side as he sits sadly in the ruined chapel, and later he can let himself go a bit in his song, 'Sighing Softly to the River'. I used to put in a touch of ballet here, which was nicely incongruous for such a military character.

Now I've dealt with the older characters, the rest are a bit of a mixture. First there's Ko-Ko – he's a one-off, requiring a 'stage Japanese' make-up, the base very slightly olive, the eyebrows and eyelines a definite black to match his wig. And while I'm on the subject of wigs, do watch those joins! My Ko-Ko wig had a very high forehead of chamois leather, ending in a net band which was, I hope, invisible once it was stuck down with spirit gum and covered with greasepaint. And it had to be greasepaint. Pancake, I found, wouldn't do the job. I used to block out the outer part of my eyebrows, first by applying dampened soap, then when dry, greasepaint. I would then extend the eyebrow upward and outwards, bringing it down a little at the end. A black line along the top eyelid, extending it slightly beyond the natural eye gives an almond shape and an oriental appearance. I always kept a box of watercolours handy for lines and fine detail – I found them most effective. White pancake, too, is useful for blending and highlighting.

Someone once asked me what age Ko-Ko would be. I had to think hard, for I'd never considered this at all. For me, he is ageless. I suppose he must be somewhere between forty and fifty perhaps, as he's Yum-Yum's guardian. Presumably his age is one of the reasons that she doesn't fancy him, and much prefers the handsome young Nanki-Poo. But for me, Ko-Ko's just Ko-Ko, and age doesn't come into it.

I always think of him as being a small man, though I believe taller actors have played him quite successfully. Peter Pratt played him as a rather timid, slightly nervous character, but I don't see him that way. To me he is cheeky and lovable. I used to turn my toes in and take small steps, hunching my shoulders a little, and tucking my hands in my wide sleeves. This felt Japanese, and as Ko-Ko was a cheap tailor, used to being obsequious to his customers, it seemed in character.

'I've got a little list'

It seems coincidental that encores always tend to follow second act trios; *The Mikado* was no exception to that rule. 'Here's a How-de-do' inevitably received enormous applause, and at first I used Martyn Green's ideas which included fans which diminished in size, and driving the imaginary little 'car' across the stage. But, being me, I soon had to come up with some of my own. I used fans too, some of which I produced from unexpected places, including from Yum-Yum's kimono, or from her wig, as if by magic. At one time I was pulled across the stage on a small truck, knitting madly, to return almost at once with the finished product – a red and green fan, complete with spokes, which I had previously constructed. All good fun. But even Ko-Ko has his moment of pathos as all comedians should, of course. This came in 'Tit Willow', which I sang perfectly straight, out front, as if I was singing to the bird himself. I would suggest to all prospective Ko-Ko's, focus on a spot in the auditorium, up in the circle perhaps, *see* the little bird perched there on his branch – picture his small sad face, and sing to *him*. I think you'll find it will work. I believe it did for me.

My first *Gondoliers* as an understudy featured the Duke of Plaza-Toro in the Charles Ricketts design, with full white curled wig, requiring a pale rather exaggerated make-up with emphasis on eyes and lips and a beauty spot. In 1957 sets and costumes were redesigned by Peter Goffin, and the Duke appeared in altogether bolder colours and dark wig, which called for a more Spanish-oriented make-up. Then Luciana Arrighi was called upon to redesign costumes in 1968 and I found myself elegantly Edwardian – silver haired, with a neat beard, so then I returned to the paler make-up. Anthony Besch came to direct this new production, and it was the one I enjoyed most though I found the Duke's first act costume too smart for its impoverished wearer. There were, I believe, mixed reactions to my eating spaghetti during Don Alhambra's song, 'I stole the Prince', and I was uneasy about it myself, for there was inevitably laughter at this point. Ken and I got together and worked out how this business could be done to his advantage, and I kept it to a minimum, timing it so that I had a long piece of spaghetti hanging from my mouth during a pause. Ken turned to look at me disapprovingly and I sucked it up quickly; that got a laugh for both of us and I did not feel that I was upstaging him. It wasn't an easy piece of business, but we made it work.

Patience and *Ruddigore* did not occur so frequently in the repertoire as the more obviously popular operas, but they were two of my favourites. I really enjoyed playing Bunthorne and went to town with his make-up, with a pale base, a small curved black moustache and tiny pointed beard. My wig was excellent – black, with a dramatic white streak. I must state most emphatically the importance of *eyes* on stage; if they are not sufficiently emphasised, they simply will not register from the front. Surely men can't wear mascara? some of you may ask. Let me state categorically that they most certainly can! And should. It is surprising what a difference darkened lashes can make. Try it. I even experimented with false eyelashes, which weighed down my lids slightly, giving them a languid look. Bunthorne, as he says himself, is an aesthetic sham. He is a poseur. Everything he says is studied, every movement calculated and rehearsed until it achieves perfection. He enjoys the adoration of the crowd of lovesick maidens who pursue him relentlessly, and is filled with jealousy when Grosvenor appears on the scene, threatening to usurp his position. Having just described Bunthorne's every movement as 'calculated' reminds me of one occasion when mine were most certainly not! I was just entering on the introduction to 'Am I alone and unobserved' when my feet shot from under me and I fell smack on my bottom with a loud 'Ooops!' Not at all in character, but it got such a laugh from the audience, and from that moment I could do nothing wrong – they were with me till the end of the show. I don't advise anyone to try that, however.

Another fall I had in *Patience* was at the end of the duet 'Sing boo to you', when I jumped up into Christene Palmer's arms (she was my Lady Jane) as usual, for her to carry me off. On this occasion she dropped me – I fell on the base of my spine, and it really hurt. We had to go on immediately for the encore, and I just could not stand up. Still, I thought, the show must go on, so I crawled back on to the stage and did the encore on all fours. The audience must have thought the whole thing was intentional, and they laughed and applauded like mad. I didn't repeat that particular encore, nevertheless.

When I first played King Gama in *Princess Ida* it seemed that Miss Carte thought I was much too nice. To tell the truth, I was sorry for the little old man with a hump on his back, whom everyone hated, and consequently I was playing him too sympathetically. Well, if they want Gama played more evilly, they shall have it, I thought. My wig was dirtied and I lined my face to make me look bad tempered, that was a start. Then I altered my voice to a cracked, unpleasant sound – screamed and whined in a cantankerous way. It was tough on the vocal cords, and I began to get what I called my 'Gama throat' after every performance of *Princess Ida*. But it worked, I think. At least, nobody could say any more that I was too nice.

King Gama *Princess Ida*

I enjoyed playing Robin Oakapple in *Ruddigore,* and the opportunity of changing character and make-up for Sir Ruthven Murgatroyd in Act II. Robin was – at least, where Rose Maybud was concerned – 'diffident, modest and shy'. He needs, as a young farmer, to have a healthy make-up and to look as attractive as possible. I had a very nice chestnut brown wig which suited the character well. Robin is bashful where Rose Maybud is concerned, and this is especially

Robin Oakapple. *Ruddigore*

obvious in their first scene and duet. A startling change comes over him in Act II, when after being revealed as the bad Sir Ruthven Murgatroyd he must change make-up and costume to fit his new identity. Of course, he is still the old Robin under this frightening new exterior, and the transformation is mainly visual. Harsh lines added to the make-up will achieve this, and a new more melodramatic manner. A hasty return to the former Robin has to be made before the finale. There are no opportunities in *Ruddigore* for encores or dancing, but in a different way it's just as enjoyable as any of the other operas.

The Sorcerer, Gilbert and Sullivan's first full-length opera (not counting *Thespis)* was given a new production in 1971. This was the first time the opera had been seen since the sets and costumes had been destroyed in the London blitz, so I suppose I can say that – as far as the audiences of that time were concerned – I created the role of John Wellington Wells, the Sorcerer himself. It was a challenge to be confronted with a brand new part to learn, rehearse and perform, and one which required me to grapple with what must be the greatest tongue-twister of all time – 'My name is John Wellington Wells'.

Wells is an interesting character, and quite different from any I had played so far. Michael Heyland, who was directing the new production, thought it might be a good idea to make him a Cockney – after all, his emporium of magic is situated at 'Number seventy Simmery Axe' which is in the heart of the City of London, and well within the sound of Bow bells. He is really a Victorian 'spiv' or 'wide boy', will sell anything to anybody, and knows exactly what he's doing. I wore a longish wig, bald on top, with a kiss curl and sideburns, and a jaunty moustache that curled up at the ends. My eyebrows swept upwards, and I looked smart and dapper in a slightly brash way. The Cockney approach suited the character very nicely, I thought. To anyone attempting Wells in this way, I advise a careful study of the accent. Find a real Cockney, or someone who really knows how to coach you – nothing's worse than a bad accent – better do it straight if there's any doubt.

The Sorcerer

There's one character left – Jack Point. To me, he's quite apart from all the others. There is a real chance to act here, both comedy, and more especially, tragedy. There is so much of Jack Point in my own character and I find it easy to identify with him. He is deeply in love with Elsie, whom he hopes to marry, and he must make this clear throughout. There has to be an obvious bond between them which is not always apparent in some productions, and if it is not, an important element of their relationship is lacking.

Jack Point must look as attractive as you can make him. As he is constantly on the road from one place to another, he may be slightly tanned, but though he is inevitably shabby, he tries to put on as good an appearance as he can for his audience. After all, if he fails to attract any spectators, there will be no money, so he does his best with the meagre resources at his disposal. When I played Jack Point my opening costume was fairly drab, but jaunty, and I wore a boot on one foot and a shoe on the other. I often pondered on the reason for this, and decided that perhaps once he had two boots, but one wore out and he could not afford another, so got a shoe instead! One day Miss Carte was in front, watching *Yeomen* and complained that 'Mr Reed's shoes are scuffed' whereupon I was given new ones. I thought this was ridiculous. Of course Jack Point's shoes were scuffed, – how could they not be, with all the use they had, and no money to buy any more? I soon made my new ones scuffed again.

I found it so easy to break down in tears at the end, when I saw that I had lost Elsie for ever. All I had to do as I stood waiting in the wings to make my last entrance was to think of something sad, and I was away. But I soon learned to be careful and keep my feelings under control – it's impossible to sing if a sob comes at the wrong time. I remember having to do two shows of *Yeomen* on a matinee day and thinking I couldn't go through all that agony twice, so I resorted to glycerine tears at the afternoon performance. To my amazement Beryl Dixon, who was then in the chorus, came to me as the curtain fell, eyes streaming, and said, 'Oh, John, you really got it today!' So there you are, aspiring Jack Points, glycerine will sometimes do the trick, but you must convey the emotion as well.

Does Jack Point die of a broken heart? That's the question everyone asks. I think every member of the audience must make up his own mind about that. My own personal opinion is that he collapses, ('falls insensible' according to Gilbert), recovers, but gradually loses the will to live without Elsie, and just fades away. But that's only my idea – everyone has their own.

Looking back over my twenty years spent playing these parts I always think how lucky I was to have the chance to play them over and over again. I became so accustomed to the costumes that they felt like part of me – putting them on felt like putting on the character they represented. I became Ko-Ko or Bunthorne or Jack Point as soon as I was dressed and made up. I believe the 'Grossmith roles' are some of the greatest ever written, and I am proud to have had the chance of getting to know all those wonderful characters so intimately.

Jack Point
The Yeomen of the Guard

CHAPTER 12

'. . . a regular royal Queen' *(The Gondoliers)*

One of the pleasantest features of playing the roles I so long enjoyed was that you got to meet a great many interesting people, from Queen Elizabeth II to Queen Passionella (alias Danny La Rue!).

I had the honour of meeting the Queen many times. She would sometimes attend a performance unannounced, though rumours of her presence usually circulated during the evening. At the end of the show we would be requested to wait on stage, and she would be brought up to meet us. She was always very charming, but seemed rather shy. When it was my turn to be presented, I'm sure I was more at ease than she was, and certainly had a lot more to say!

Meeting Her Majesty the Queen

During the company's 1959 London season, when I was still fairly new to the roles, I was in my dressing room at the Princes Theatre (now the Shaftesbury) when Beti Lloyd Jones came in and said, 'Prince Charles is in front tonight.' I didn't believe her at first, but she said, 'He *is* – you can just about see him, in the front row of the dress circle.' It was *The Mikado* that evening, and as soon as I had the opportunity I glanced up at the circle, and there he was. I could see a line of grown-ups, then a smaller figure with rather prominent ears. I believe he was about ten at that time. At the end of the show I was taking off my make-up and my face was covered with grease when there was a knock at the door. Thinking it was one of the company, I yelled in my best King Gama voice, 'Come in if you're pretty!' and went on with what I was doing. I turned round to see Prince Charles with Miss Peebles, and Commander Campbell, I think it was, standing in my very tatty dressing room. I was at a momentarily at a loss for words (unusual for me!) so I asked him if he had enjoyed the show. 'Yes, very much,' he replied. 'Are you coming to see any of the other operas?' I asked. 'I don't know,' he said, looking eagerly at Miss Peebles, who smiled sweetly and answered. 'We shall have to see.' I had to stop myself from saying, 'Why don't you ask your mother? I can pick you up and take you back afterwards – I pass your house on my way to the theatre.' But I could hardly say that to the heir to the throne! I asked him about the different characters in *The Mikado*, and he said, 'I thought Katisha was terrible – she was so ugly!' 'Ah,' I replied, 'that's just her make-up – she's really a very pretty lady – I'll ask her to come and meet you.' So Gillian Knight was summoned to Prince Charles's presence, and he was astonished to see that she was indeed most attractive in real life. Gillian and I were, and still are, very good friends, and I thought she might like this opportunity of meeting the young prince.

Chatting with the Duke of Edinburgh

It was a number of years before I met him again, this time with the Queen and Prince Philip, and it was another *Mikado* at the Saville Theatre. The Royal party were in the circle bar, and the cast were to be presented to them one by one during the interval. This involved going out of the stage door entering through another door, and after the presentation, exiting through another, descending some stairs and making our way through the audience, who were milling about in the foyer – a very unusual procedure. After a pleasant conversation with the Queen and Prince Philip I passed along the line and saw Prince Charles, whom I hadn't realised was present. He was pointing at me as I approached, and said, 'Let me see, it's six years since I saw you last.' And he was right – he remembered his visit to my dressing room.

The Queen Mother was always charming, and I met her a number of times. One occasion that remains in my memory was at Her Majesty's Theatre in Aberdeen when Mr Cocker, of Cockers Roses, Edinburgh, who was a friend of mine, had given five thousand yellow roses to decorate the theatre – it looked magnificent. At the fall of the curtain the Queen Mother was brought on to the stage to meet us, and the usual procedure followed. She walked along the front row of principals, and then was supposed to meet the next line-up, which consisted mainly of management and staff. The chorus stood at the back, and seeing them there, she said, 'I want to speak to those people,' whereupon she broke through the lines and went to talk to them. I thought that was a wonderful thing to do, and absolutely typical of her caring nature. She made sure she had a word with everyone, then waved to us all as she went out. That wasn't the last we saw of her, for she popped her head round the flat for a last cheery wave before she finally left.

In Jubilee year, 1977, the company travelled down to Windsor to present *HMS Pinafore* by royal command to the Queen and the royal family. (I was amused to see ourselves described in the programme as 'Her Majesty's servants'!) We made up at trestle tables in a great room with screened-off sections, and how we laughed at the china jugs and basins provided for us for our ablutions, emblazoned with the letter 'V'. It occurred to me that these very same utensils must have been in use when the D'Oyly Carte performed *The Gondoliers* for Queen Victoria way back in March 1891, 'plus ça change' I thought. Maybe I was sitting in the chair that Frank Wyatt used, for it was he who was playing the Duke at that performance, and not George Grossmith, who had left by then. I remember that Angus Ogilvie popped his head round the door, saw what was going on, winked at me and hastily withdrew. Quite a bit of rehearsal was required as we adapted ourselves to our unusual venue. Crossing backstage was quite a complicated affair; you had to make an exit one side and rush along a wide marble corridor flanked by suits of armour to make your entrance from the other side of the stage. This was rather tricky where the encores were concerned, and the sight of the dignified Sir Joseph Porter running for dear life in such gracious surroundings must have been quite extraordinary.

After the show, which our illustrious audience appeared to have enjoyed enormously, the chorus were allowed to go and change, while the principals were requested to remain to meet the royals. The Queen Mother came to me, and was immediately concerned for my welfare; 'Oh, you've got nothing to drink,' she said with great concern, summoning a flunkey to provide me with a glass of wine. I was touched by her thoughtfulness – it was just the thing my own mother would have done. Nobody ever came into our house without immediately being offered a cup of tea and a piece of cake. 'I love all that wonderful music,' she said, beaming. She had obviously enjoyed the show, and didn't mind showing it. A number of the royal family were there that night; I remember seeing Princess Margaret and the Ogilvies, and I had quite an amusing chat with Prince Philip. 'How long do you have to tour each year?' he asked. 'Most of the time,' I replied, 'with just four weeks holiday.' 'That's hard work,' he said. 'Oh, yes' I agreed, 'but then, there's no peace for the wicked.' The Prince laughed wryly. 'Don't I know it!' he answered.

The principals were eventually released to remove make-up and change, after which we made our way to another room where refreshments were to be provided – or at least that's what we thought. By the time we arrived the chorus and orchestra were all seated comfortably at tables, and there was not a scrap of food left, or indeed, anywhere to sit. Mr Lloyd came up to me beaming, obviously delighted with how things had gone. 'Everything all right, John?' he asked. 'No, it's not!' I answered crossly. 'The principals have worked their socks off this evening to make the show a success, we stay behind to chat to the royal family, arrive here at last for refreshments and somewhere to relax, and there's nothing to eat and nowhere to sit down anyway!' I myself wasn't bothered about eating, but I was concerned on behalf of my fellow principals at the shabby treatment we were receiving. Surely a table and some refreshments could have been set aside for the few of us who has been delayed by doing their bit for the company? Freddie Lloyd had nothing to say, but then, he never had in that sort of situation. 'They're bringing out some strawberries and cream now, John,' he said, 'Why don't you go and get some?' I looked across to the counter and saw an enormous queue forming. 'If you think I'm going to fight for a few strawberries, you're very much mistaken,' I said. 'I shall go and buy myself a whole basket tomorrow and eat them all.'

It's always said that there were no stars in the D'Oyly Carte, and I'm quite happy with that idea. After all, I spent eight years in the chorus, know what valuable work they do, and respect them very much. Many principals started out as choristers, though there were quite a few who preferred to forget that fact – I never did. But there were occasions when we could have been given a little more consideration, for sometimes we had to meet important people, do press interviews, appear on radio and television programmes, and consequently arrived later than the rest of the company at a given venue. Windsor Castle was one example of the management's thoughtless treatment of principal artists, and there were many others. I would often arrive at a hotel during one of our American tours to find myself at the end of a long queue at reception, yet I would be required to attend a press interview as soon as possible. Nothing was done to help me find my room and prepare myself for this. I would have to wait my turn and watch as dissatisfied members of the chorus would come back and demand to change rooms before I ever got to the head of the queue. I eventually took whatever room was left, relieved to get anything at all. To my mind, this was simply not acceptable when the appointments I was hurrying to keep were entirely for the company's benefit. Nevertheless that was the way the D'Oyly Carte worked, and it seemed that no complaints or objections would ever have changed it. In any case, I hated making a fuss, and tended to let things ride. Perhaps I should have taken a firmer stand, but it's not in my nature to do so.

Sharing a joke with one time Prime Minister Harold Wilson

Prime Minister Harold Wilson was a firm Gilbert and Sullivan fan, and I met him a couple of times, the first occasion being after a performance of the new *Sorcerer* in 1971. He made a beeline for me and embarked on a long discussion about the operas. Every time I tried to disengage myself he held firmly on to my arm and prevented me from leaving, delighted to have the chance of a good chat about his beloved G&S with someone who was so closely associated with it. I was to meet him again at a reception at the British embassy in Washington on one of our American tours, and the same thing occurred. He just loved the Savoy operas, and I should think he quite probably played a major part in my being awarded the OBE four years later. The actor Donald Sinden was another enthusiast, and used to come to performances at the Savoy, popping round to visit me in my dressing room afterwards. I always had the room on stage level, which was where the principal comedian had always dressed, then one year, for some unaccountable reason I was allocated a room on the next floor, with Kenneth Sandford. On the first day of the season I had gone running down to my usual dressing room, to find two of the principal ladies already installed there. I was puzzled and not a little hurt at my strange demotion, but how could I go to the stage manager and demand that they be evicted, when they were two of my friends? So, being me, and hating any fuss, I had to grin and bear it. Danny la Rue turned up on one of the first nights, came back to see me and made his usual grand entrance. 'Whatever are you doing up here?' he asked in amazement. I shrugged my shoulders. What could I say? There was no accounting for some of the management's peculiar actions, but they caused unnecessary resentment at times.

While on this particular subject of dressing rooms, there was a time at the Theatre Royal, Brighton, when I arrived a little later than usual on the opening night, to find that, owing to limited dressing accommodation, all the male principals were in one room. Everyone else was there already, and there was absolutely nowhere to set out my make-up, let alone sit down in front of a mirror to put it on. I looked around in disbelief, and saw John Webley, a young and talented baritone, standing at the mantelpiece, trying to put his make-up on. He had recently been very ill – in fact we were to lose him in all too short a time, and although I find it hard to make a fuss for myself, I had no qualms in speaking up when I saw what John was having to cope with. I called the stage manager. 'Look,' I said, 'how am I supposed to make up? I've nowhere to sit down, even. I simply can't go on tonight under these conditions.' And what did the stage manager say? No apologies, no attempts to rectify the situation, just 'Very well, I'll put your understudy on.' It so happened that Freddie Lloyd had come down with Dame Bridget that night, so I summoned him. The result was that the conductor vacated his room, which was then given to me. 'And John Webley can come too,' I said, which he did, much to his relief. But why cause so much anguish and discomfort to artists who are about to go on and do a show? I shall never understand the workings of that company. Oh dear, I've just realised I've just done quite a bit of grumbling – I'd better stop now or I shall have to shall have to change the title of this book!

CHAPTER 13

'. . . Everything is a source of fun' *(The Mikado)*

You might think this chapter is a series of disjointed jottings, and you'd be right. Anecdotes and reminiscences don't pop into your mind in an orderly fashion. It's impossible to put them into neat categories, so I shall make this into a kaleidoscope of memories and tell the stories just as they occur to me.

One occasion I recall clearly was when Sir Winston and Lady Churchill, accompanied by Viscount Montgomery, came to see a performance of *The Gondoliers* at the Princes Theatre. I was still in the chorus then, and playing Antonio, which meant that I spent quite a lot of time at the front, stage right, during the opening scene. The famous guests were sitting in the first row of the stalls at that side, so I had a really good view of them. Winston would turn to his wife at intervals, and I could hear him asking her questions about what was going on, quite audibly, in that famous voice of his. I had just sung 'For the merriest fellows are we,' and danced across the front and he pointed straight at me: 'Who's that?' he wanted to know. At the interval the party were escorted to a private room for refreshments or, more importantly, for Sir Winston's brandy. The great man was seated, glass in hand when Bruce Worsley, our company manager, enquired, 'Soda, sir?' Sir Winston nodded, Bruce reached for the syphon, but at that moment someone asked a question. Winston turned to answer just as Bruce squirted the soda, missing the glass completely, with the result that Winston received the full force of the soda in his lap. The interval over, act two was due to begin and we were all standing waiting on stage. Goddie was ready to start, but still nothing happened. The audience were getting restless, there were voices from the upper circle shouting, 'Come on, Winnie!' Eventually he appeared, to tremendous cheers, and when he reached his seat he turned and gave the audience his customary 'V' sign. We learned later that the delay was caused by 'Winnie' having to have his trousers dried before he could reappear for the second act!

There's another Churchill story connected to that evening. Harry Haste was our stage carpenter at the time, though to call him just that is something of an understatement. He was responsible for absolutely everything concerned with getting in and out of the theatre, scenery, props, and transport from one venue to another, and that included foreign tours. Harry was a large man in every sense of the word, slow-moving, with a dry sense of humour and a voice like gravel. He was always a great one for telling jokes, and whenever I repeat one of his I always feel I must deliver the punch line in Harry's gravelly tones. He was undoubtably one of the really great characters of those far-off D'Oyly Carte days.

Harry knew, of course, of Sir Winston's expected attendance at the theatre that night, and had somehow managed to acquire a Rolls Royce for the occasion. Timed to perfection, the Rolls glided to a halt at the front of the theatre, where Bruce Worsley and his assistant, Michael Freshwater, were waiting, rehearsed and keyed up for the great event. As the opulent limousine stopped in front of them they approached it obsequiously, seeing in the back the unmistakable figure complete with black homberg and cigar. 'Good evenin' sir,' said Bruce (he always left off his final 'g's') as the chauffeur opened the door. From the interior of the car came those unmistakably gravelly tones, 'What the bloody hell do you want?'

Yes, it was Harry, of course, he was never one to spare any expense where a good laugh was concerned. They don't make them like that anymore.

A comical thing happened at a performance of *Pirates* during one of our London seasons. I was in the chorus then, and on stage with the rest of the pirates, ready for the opening chorus as the overture ended to the usual applause. The introduction to the opera began, then the curtain rose – at least, it rose about three feet. To our surprise it stayed suspended thus for some time, so we had to get down on the floor and sing through the narrow gap, as the music was continuing and it seemed the only thing to do! Some of us were kneeling, others bending down, and a few more uninhibited chaps were rolling about on the floor as if they'd already had too much pirate sherry. Of course, we were laughing like mad, so were the audience, though I suspect Goddie wasn't too pleased.

Another very funny incident (though not for the victim!) happened one night, again in *Pirates*. One of the baritone choristers, who was in the habit of criticising all the principals and inferring that he could do so much better, understudied the role of Samuel, and had to go on one night. All went fairly well until the part in the second act where he is distributing the implements to the rest of the pirates for the raid on Tremorden Castle. This section lies vocally rather high for Samuel anyway, but this poor chap pitched it an octave higher still! The result was fairly amazing and the rest of us were suppressing wild giggles as we witnessed his struggles. As soon as he was able to make an exit, he marched straight round to the prompt corner and relinquished his Samuel understudy on the spot.

When performing a show over and over again, the dialogue becomes second nature to you, and any slight departure from the correct words comes as quite a shock. I remember a hysterical incident in *The Mikado* in act two – when Pooh-Bah, Pitti-Sing and Ko-Ko are prostrated before The Mikado. Pooh-Bah (played by Ken Sandford) had the line, 'No, of course we couldn't tell who the gentleman really was,' and Pitti-Sing should have said, 'It wasn't written on his forehead, you know.' On this particular night, Peggy Ann Jones, who was playing Pitti-Sing, said for some unaccountable reason, 'It wasn't written on *any* part of his anatomy, you know,' whereupon we all collapsed, shaking and helpless with laughter. How I ever got my next line out I'll never know.

The Mikado seemed to come in for more than its fair share of funny moments – probably because it was performed more often than the other operas. In one of the productions the girls were lined up along the front of the stage, kneeling with their backs to the audience for the Mikado's song, so were able to indulge in all sorts of discreet jokes. As they knelt down their kimonos would tend to come open and expose the odd knee, but on one occasion when I had to run on and say, 'I am honoured in being permitted to welcome your Majesty' etc., I was confronted by an whole array of bare knees inscribed with rude messages! That reminds me of an occasion in *Pirates* when Beryl Dixon had made her two rather plump knees to look like twin babies, complete with features. She had put on a pair of frilly pantaloons, the lace trimming looking for all the world like bonnets framing their faces! None of this frivolity, of course, was ever visible to the audience, and we had grown accustomed to keeping straight faces against tremendous odds, which was absolutely essential!

At another performance of *The Mikado,* again during his entrance, the Mikado, played by John Ayldon on this occasion, had to walk along the line of girls in the course of his song, and one night was quite alarmed as he suddenly felt something fastened round his ankles. I thought his movements seemed rather more restrained than usual, and when it was possible to do so, he whispered to me, 'I think they've tied my legs together – can you see what it is, John?' I found a moment to do this, and discovered it was just a pair of bicycle clips, invisible beneath his baggy trousers!

During my years in the chorus, at a performance of *Princess Ida,* when the men storm Castle Adamant in act two, we all rushed in and the ramp collapsed. Now, I was fairly agile and managed to scramble my way up to where I was supposed to be, to find myself all alone. So there was this little fella singing 'Oh, I love the jolly rattle of an ordeal by battle' in glorious isolation, with the rest of the men singing in the wings, unable to get on. I must have looked ridiculous – my costume was crazy enough anyway, with one black leg and one white one, and the opposite way round for the sleeves. Topped by a black pillbox hat with felt antlers, I must have looked like a diminutive 'Monarch of the Glen' perched up there alone on that rock, singing to all those women!

The Gondoliers had its share of funny moments. One night as the Ducal party was making its grand entrance in the gondola, the wretched thing got stuck and stopped suddenly with a tremendous jolt. In that particular production we carried a picnic basket, and this overturned, filling our laps with bottles, sandwiches, cups and all manner of things. We had to pick them up hastily in order to get out of the gondola and were forced to make our entrance carrying all this paraphernalia. I had my fingers through several cup handles, a bottle under my arm, and goodness knows what else. The others were similarly encumbered, and in that state we endeavoured to sing the opening number. It was some time before I was able to dispose of these unwanted props down a convenient 'well', and they made a loud clang as they fell to the bottom. What the others did, I really don't know. What I do know is that we sang our individual lines with increasing hysteria, and when it got to Phillip Potter's line as Luiz, all we heard was an incoherent mumbling as he struggled in vain to sing anything at all.

One night during *Ruddigore* I was standing in the wings and noticed a big pile of boxes nearby. In one of my mischievous moods, I waited till Ken Sandford as Sir Despard said the words, 'But soft, someone comes' then I pushed them over. There was one hell of a crash. Ken timed his dialogue perfectly and there was an enormous laugh from the audience. But I received a letter from Bridget asking me to take out that piece of business, so of course I did. A week or so later I received a letter asking me if I'd mind putting back again. Apparently the management had been inundated with complaints from the audience about its omission!

I have already mentioned the necessity of making sure there is no sign of a wrinkle in your stockings when playing such parts as Sir Joseph Porter, and I found that one of the best methods of ensuring this is to use a lady's suspender belt to keep them up, wearing it inside out so that the suspender buttons are not prominent. When we were playing Manchester on one of our tours I decided I could do with a couple of new ones, and I'd noticed a shop selling corsetry on the outskirts of the city, near where I was staying. I went in and said to one of the assistants, 'I want a suspender belt, please.' 'What size sir?' she asked. 'I'm not quite sure,' I replied, 'it's for me.' She was rather taken aback at this, but brought out a selection for me to see. I then explained what I wanted it for, and she had a good laugh. Soon, three other assistants came to join in, and were holding up various flimsy garments. 'Here's a black lacy one,' said one, and 'Oh, here's one with rosebuds!' laughed another. I eventually departed with two very plain, servicable suspender belts, amidst much laughter. I don't think those girls had ever had such an entertaining time, or such an unusual customer!

I'll never forget one of our company parties – I think it was at Sadler's Wells, when we all dressed up. Jon Ellison, who played many of the small baritone roles, and who in my eyes was an invaluable member of the company, was persuaded by Julia Goss to put on a pair of fishnet tights, a mini-skirt and an eccentric wig. The final touch was a sash proclaiming him to be 'Miss D'Oyly Carte.' He had very muscular, masculine legs, which looked ridiculous in those tights, and the whole effect was extraordinary. Bridget never came to any of our parties, they weren't her scene at all. But never say 'never'. Jon made a flamboyant entrance and came face to face with the lady herself! She had decided, quite uncharacteristically, to put in an appearance at the last moment. Poor Jon was absolutely horrified, but I'm sure she took it in the right way – she had quite a sense of humour on the quiet.

There are lots of tales of petticoats and frilly drawers falling down on stage, when elastic has given way or tapes have come undone, and most can be surreptitiously disposed of. But trust Peggy Ann Jones to make a feature of such an incident! It happened in *Pirates,* when for some reason or other Peggy's pantaloons concertinaed round her ankles. At a suitable moment she discreetly stepped out of them, and Jon Ellison was able to pick them up and throw them, as he thought, into the wings. It seems that his aim was not as accurate as he could have wished, for instead of the rejected drawers disappearing without trace, they caught on a piece of scenery and hung there for the rest of the act like a strange item of laundry. The effect of this on the company I leave to your imagination.

I had a very strange experience in *The Mikado* once; as the chorus leave the stage in act two after Pooh-Bah's verse in the trio, singing, 'But in this case it all took place exactly as he says,' I moved across the stage to find two eggs had been left on the floor in the exact place I was going to stand. I managed to roll one into the floats, but was obliged to pocket the other. The question was: were they hard-boiled? I fervently hoped so! The opera proceeded, and I forgot about the egg in my pocket until the curtain call. I took it out and as I took Katisha's hand (I believe it was Lyndsie Holland) I put it gently into her palm. She smiled at me rather suspiciously; by now

I assumed the egg must be hard-boiled so I squeezed her hand, and horror – there was an ominous crunching sound as the raw egg broke and its sticky contents ran all over our hands and on to the stage. What a mess – it was a good job the curtain came down at that moment!

All this sounds as if we spent most of our time laughing and playing jokes, but that wasn't the case at all. A great deal of hard, serious work was involved in all those years of touring, and in actual fact the jokes and funny incidents were fairly few and far between. When you were doing the same operas day after day, year after year, I'm sure a bit of fun and humour gave an added sparkle to the performance. Nothing was ever allowed to interfere with the show, unless caused by an accidental happening which the audience could see for themselves and join in the fun – such as my fall when I made my entrance as Bunthorne, for instance. In all my years with the D'Oyly Carte, my main purpose was to please the audience and send them away smiling and happy at the end of the show. And I believe we did just that.

CHAPTER 14

'Shreds and patches . . .' *(The Mikado)*

I was in Washington DC on the D'Oyly Carte's 1978 American tour when I received a phone call from New York asking if I would be willing to appear on the Dick Cavett Show. His secretary said it would be an interview lasting about an hour, with a couple of numbers from the operas if I was willing. I knew this was a very popular television show, and could see that it would be a good bit of publicity, both for me and for the company. 'Fine,' I agreed. 'And Mr Cavett would like to sing a duet with you,' she added. 'Certainly,' I replied, 'which one?' I was amazed when she said, 'He would like to do the Nightmare Song.' Good heavens, I thought, how on earth would that be possible? 'He suggests that you sing four lines, then he will sing the next four, and so on,' she explained. 'Well,' I told her, 'if he's game, then so am I.'

On April 26th I left for New York on an early train with David Mackie, who was to accompany us, and there we met Dick Cavett, a charming, dapper little man, even smaller than I, and I am only five feet seven inches tall. I soon discovered that he was a genuine Gilbert and Sullivan fan. 'I used to bore the pants off my parents when I was a little boy, always jumping onto a chair and singing the patter songs,' he laughed. We soon got to work, and it was fun, that version of the Nightmare Song, four lines in that American drawl of his, then my four, trying to pick up the tempo in time for him to drag it back again. I was glad to have David at the piano – the idiosyncrasies of our performance didn't seem to put him out in the least and I don't think I've ever enjoyed that song so much! Of course we did an encore of 'When I was a lad' from *Pinafore,* in much the same way, with me giving Dick a dig in the ribs when it was his turn to sing. I very much enjoyed meeting Dick Cavett, he was a great host, and the whole programme was fun.

Of course, there were many press, radio and television interviews during our tours of the USA – most are forgotten but one or two of them remain clearly in my memory, and the funniest one of all is when I was awarded a temporary knighthood! The company was in Los Angeles and I was asked to do a radio interview in Hollywood – they would send a cab for me, so I agreed. I arrived at the large imposing studio and was shown in, made welcome and provided with coffee. There was a glass recording studio partitioned off and I could see a young woman sitting there, talking and playing records of classical music – it was a little like our Classic FM, I suppose. Eventually I was taken in and seated in a chair next to her. She told me quietly that the last record was being played and when it ended she had one or two announcements to make, and would then introduce me. After a few moments she smiled at me, and said in tones of awe: 'I have with me today a gentleman who has been awarded the O.B.E by the Queen Of England – *Sir* John Reed!

To say I was flabbergasted at my sudden elevation in rank would be putting it mildly – my mouth dropped open and I wondered whether to intervene. My host was continuing with her introduction, and the programme was going out live, so I decided I'd have to let it go, hoping that my spurious title would not be mentioned again. To explain the complications of British awards to an American audience would probably have taken the rest of the programme. But alas for my hopes – it seemed that every question she asked me included 'Sir John' – 'What did you think of that, Sir John?' 'Which is your favourite part, Sir John?' etc. etc. And so it went on, to the end of the interview. She was a delightful person, and I couldn't possibly have pointed out her mistake without causing her terrible embarrassment. I hoped that none of the company had been listening. I was very touched when my charming host presented me with avocado pears and exotic fruit and flowers which she had brought from her garden. 'May I see you to your cab?' she asked, and escorted me across a green to where it was waiting for me. 'Thank you so much, Sir John,' she said, 'it was a wonderful interview. Do come again next time you're in Los Angeles.' She put out her hand, and as I took it, dropped into a grateful curtsey. I just didn't know what to do – I got into the cab, waved goodbye and sank back into my seat. I was hysterical – I don't think I've ever laughed so much, or so loudly. The cab driver must have thought I was mad.

A few days later I had another radio interview which I was not looking forward to very much. I had been warned that the woman who was coming to talk to me was rather 'difficult' and I would probably not enjoy it. I was staying at a very nice hotel just behind Grauman's Chinese Theatre, which consisted of apartments grouped round a swimming pool. The lady arrived, and we sat down to talk. She asked what I had done before the D'Oyly Carte and I said, 'Well, really I'm only a butcher's son from the north of England.' Before I could continue, she exclaimed, 'Oh that's wonderful!' And from that moment we got on like a house on fire, laughing and drinking coffee and generally having a good time. Apparently she was used to interviewing the 'stars' who only wanted to exaggerate the great things they'd done – Mae West was one – and she was relieved to find at last a *real* person who was quite happy to talk about his humble beginnings.

Goddie and I went together to be interviewed one day, and were asked to go in separately. The door was left open and I could hear all that was going on. I was alarmed at the difficult questions Goddie was being asked, all about Gilbert and Sullivan, their private lives and the history of the operas. Goodness, I thought, I couldn't answer any of those – I know the operas well enough, and all about the parts I play, but that's as far as it goes. When it was my turn to go in I allowed the interviewer to introduce me and ask a question, then I was off – I never stopped talking, and didn't give him a chance to say another word till it was time to stop. He shut his notebook of unasked questions. 'You're an easy one to interview.' he commented.

At the end of each D'Oyly Carte London season came the famous last night performance. When I first joined the company in 1951 it had been a simple occasion, maybe the overture from one of the operas followed by two acts from different ones. But gradually over the years those last nights had developed into gala performances, with crazy costumes and jokes galore. Nobody ever gave away what they intended to do, and there were always many unexpected surprises. I played Bunthorne as a 'flower power' person in the sixties when all that sort of thing was going on, so it was off to Carnaby Street to see what outrageous costume I could find. I went into a suitable shop and asked for a pair of flowered trousers. I could see the assistant raise his eyebrows at my request, for I was of rather a different age group from his usual clientele, and he produced a fairly restrained pair for me to see. 'Oh, *no,*' I said, 'I want something much more flamboyant!' He gave me a knowing look and said in a confidential tone, 'You'd better come downstairs.' I got exactly what I wanted down there, and completed my outfit with a bouffant green wig. Christene Palmer, my Lady Jane, dressed in a long floral outfit, so we made a good pair in our duet. For another last night I decided to make Bunthorne a punk, all in leathers, with a multi-coloured wig. I swaggered down to the front of the stage, chewing, and bared my chest. Written across it in bold green letters was 'BARCLAYS', for at that time they were sponsoring the D'Oyly Carte.

On another of the last nights we were doing the second act of *Ruddigore* and John Ayldon as Sir Roderic was cursing me, wearing a great gorilla hand. I was determined not to laugh, but John made a wild gesture, throwing up his arm dramatically, and the hand shot off, soaring high into the air for all to see. Well, that was it, I was done for, absolutely helpless with laughter. The audience joined in – they could see what was going on, and loved it.

Another of John Ayldon's bizarre ideas was to make his entrance as the Mikado on a horse, who promptly did its business on the stage with perfect timing. Freddie Lloyd, watching from the back of the stalls, was heard to remark, 'What a critic!' We loved those last nights – they were such fun. So did the audience, who rushed to book tickets for them almost before any of the other performances. Bridget hated them, of course.

Another joke I planned with Jon Ellison was between him as Old Adam and myself as Sir Ruthven Murgatroyd, at the beginning of act two of *Rudddigore.* I had arranged with someone to stand in the wings with a coil of rope, and when I came to the point in my speech, 'Bind him with good stout rope to yonder post,' I took the end of the rope and began to tie Jon up, winding it round and round him as I continued speaking. I had to stop frequently for laughs, but he was completely trussed up by the time I'd finished. When he came to 'It would be simply rude, nothing more. But soft, they come,' he had to make his exit with great ungainly hops. Being Jon, he made the most of it, and of course there was plenty of applause for his efforts.

Two Lord Chancellors,
Lord Hailsham & John Reed

After a performance of *Iolanthe* one evening I had the pleasure of meeting the real Lord Chancellor, who had come to see the show with the Queen Mother. 'I couldn't take my eyes off those twinkling feet,' he laughed. He had obviously enjoyed the opera very much, and he examined my costume minutely. 'I've got one like that,' he said, 'but it's not as good as yours.' He walked round me and looked at the back view. 'But I'll tell you something,' he said, 'there's a small detail missing – there should be a black rosette on the back of the cloak, at the nape of the neck.' 'I didn't know that,' I said. 'But I do know that when military uniforms are made for the stage, they mustn't be exactly authentic – there has to be something missing. Do you think it's the same for the Lord Chancellor's costume?' 'Well, it may be,' he answered, 'I don't know about that.' A few days later I was very touched to receive a small parcel, which contained a black rosette. There was a note with it, which read: 'Thank you for a scintillating performance', signed 'Elwyn Jones'. I must confess I did not attach the rosette to the back of my cloak, but had it framed – it still has pride of place on my wall, and reminds me of a delightful man and a very pleasant occasion.

I was to meet the Lord Chancellor again before long. Albert Truelove, Dame Bridget's private secretary, was asked to provide an evening's entertainment for the Bar Musical Society at Middle Temple Hall in the presence of the Queen Mother in December 1978. Cynthia Morey and Leonard Osborn were in charge of the production, which was to consist of a performance of *Trial by Jury*, followed by 'A G&S Miscellany'. Luckily it was a *Pirates* night, and I had long given up playing the Major General so was free to travel from Norwich, where the company was currently playing, to take part. I was to sing the role of the Judge, and was a little nervous of this, as I hadn't played it for quite a long time. So I was very pleased when I arrived to find many ex-D'Oyly Carte folk in the cast; Peggy Ann Jones, Mary Sansom, Mercia Glossop, Alan Barrett, Jennifer Toye – to name but a few. Barbara Lilley was to sing the Plaintiff, Geoffrey Shovelton the Defendant, Michael Tuckey, Counsel and John Broad the Usher, so I felt quite at home. Royston Nash was conducting, and there was a small ensemble of musicians to accompany us. *Trial by Jury* was the perfect choice for such an audience, and the applause was loud and long.

The Queen Mother, whom I met during the interval, was enjoying the evening hugely – she genuinely loved the operas – there was no doubt of that. I was the last to perform in the concert which comprised the second half of the programme, and it had been arranged secretly that my illustrious friend, the *real* Lord Chancellor, would come on stage and sing a duet with me – his stage counterpart from *Iolanthe.* It was 'The Law is the true embodiment of everything that's excellent' and it was an absolute riot. The audience simply would not stop applauding, and as we were going off stage, my fellow duettist said to me, 'Shall we sing it again?' 'Don't you know anything else?' I asked. 'No,' he said, so I went back on stage and announced, 'Your Majesty, Ladies and Gentlemen, I have asked the Lord Chancellor if he knows another song, and he informs me that he doesn't, so here is the same number again!'

There were drinks afterwards, and The Lord Chancellor made his way to me through the crowd. 'Thank you for looking after me, John,' he said. So I told him how I had framed his rosette, and would always treasure it. It was a great pleasure to meet such a charming and delightful man.

On one of the D'Oyly Carte American tours, when we were playing San Francisco, I had the chance to meet a film star whom I had always admired greatly. The meeting occurred in rather an extraordinary way. We were at the Geary, and next door was another theatre, the Curran, where Myrna Loy was appearing in *Barefoot in the Park*. I was putting on my make-up, and talking about her to my dresser. 'I'd love to meet her,' I said. 'OK,' he said, 'Come with me.' 'What, in this tatty old gown?' I said, 'It's all over make-up – and how shall we get to her dressing room?' I followed him as he led the way through a narrow passage which, unknown to me, linked the two theatres. We finally reached Myrna Loy's dressing room, and my dresser knocked on the door. 'Come in,' came a voice from within, and we entered. And there was Myrna Loy, the glamorous film idol of my youth, in a gown quite as tatty as mine, her hair in big rollers and her face covered with grease. She didn't care in the least, and was absolutely charming as I told her how I'd always loved her films. We chatted briefly then I had to go, as time was getting short and we both had a show to do.

After the performance one night I was getting changed when I heard a loud voice at the stage door. 'I want to go and see the funny little man!' it demanded. 'Oh, that must be me,' I thought. There was a knock at my dressing room door and a very large and flamboyant lady stood there. It was Tessie O'Shea, and she put her arms round me and gave me a great hug, which was so all-engulfing that I had quite a job finding my way out! She was on tour – with Billy Cotton, I believe – and later when we were playing NewYork Tessie came to see me again. 'I wish you'd come and visit me,' she said and gave me her address. So I called round to her apartment, which was filled with banjos. 'Music hall's dying,' she sighed. 'I used to be so popular. I make my entrance now, and all I hear is the rustling of programmes as the audience looks to see who it is.' 'But that's only because the Americans don't know you so well,' I said. 'I'm sure it's not like that at home.' Then poor Tessie started to cry. Tears rolled down her cheeks. 'I'm sorry, John,' she said, 'But I'm sad today – my partner's gone off with the hat check girl, and he's my pianist.' I tried to cheer her up, and I think I managed it a bit. I was upset to see her like that – that lady was meant for laughter, not tears.

I had a strange encounter in the States with a director who was about to put on a play on Broadway, *The Mad Woman Of Chaillot,* starring Katherine Hepburn. I can't remember his name, but he'd been to see the show, and was dead keen to get me for it. I said I was under contract to the Doyly Carte, and it would be impossible. In any case, I thought to myself, it might flop, and then where would I be? Out of work – and that was something I couldn't contemplate.

But in spite of my protestations he insisited that I should go to dinner with the backers, and unable to put up any more resistance, I agreed to this. I was subjected to a lot of persuasion – they thought they could talk me into it, but I finally refused categorically, and assumed they'd given up at last. But they had one last try – I found the script pushed under the door of my hotel room next morning!

The D'Oyly Carte made two European visits during my twenty eight years with them; the first was a brief trip to Denmark in October 1970, where we presented Th*e Mikado* and *HMS Pinafore* and the second was to Rome 1974 with *The Mikado* and *Iolanthe.* Our visit to each place lasted barely a week, and much of this time was taken up with travelling and rehearsals, so there was little leisure time. I remember being kissed on both cheeks and receiving an enormous bouquet of roses at the end of the show in Aarhus, and going through the pass door of the theatre in Copenhagen to meet the Danish royal family. In Rome, during the curtain calls for *Pinafore* I was overwhelmed when the exuberant Italian audience crowded to the front of the auditorium shouting. 'John Reed! John Reed! Bravo, John Reed!'

At this point I think I should remind myself that pride comes before a fall. I had come out of the stage door of the Theatre Royal. Newcastle, where there was quite a crowd waiting for me, and was busy signing autographs when a woman called out from the back of the crowd, 'Don't get big-headed, John Reed – I remember you in the fish shop!'

CHAPTER 15

'Can I with dignity my post resign?' *(Princess Ida)*

I had been playing the comedy roles for nearly ten years when I decided that 'all work and no play makes Johnny a dull boy,' for I was in every opera and played every matinee and every evening, eight performances a week, forty-eight weeks a year. Of course my understudy would go on for the occasional show, but this did not happen very often. And in America I would also be doing countless interviews for press, television and radio in my 'spare' time. I never saw anything of the many interesting places the company visited, as whenever I had any time to myself, which was very rare, I found it necessary to rest and prepare myself for the next show. Would it be possible to give up one of my parts, I wondered, and if so, which? The Major General was my least favourite – I decided to put it to the management. There was a lot of discussion and argument before it was finally agreed that Howard Williamson, who was then my understudy, would take over that role. Almost immediately an American tour was announced, and I looked forward to having a little free time on *Pirates* nights.

An interview with Freddie Lloyd brought swift disillusionment; it seemed that the American management were insisting that I play *all* the roles. I was so angry that at first I refused to give way. I pointed out that the role of the Major General was no longer mine, but then Mr. Lloyd gave me to understand that If I refused to play it in the States I would be putting the whole tour in jeopardy. What could I do? We came to a compromise: I would play the Major

General *only* on press nights. That should give me a little time to myself I thought.

On arriving in the States and seeing the programme, I found that *Pirates* was to be played *only* on press nights, with the exception of a couple of shows in Los Angeles. I was very angry at the false impression I had been given. When we eventually arrived in LA I decided to make the most of my limited free time. I would hire a car and drive over to Las Vegas. Most of the company seemed to have been there already, and had amazing tales to tell of what they'd seen. I mentioned my plan to my dresser, who said, 'If you've got a day off, so have I. No need to hire a car, I'll drive you over.' So I went home feeling quite relaxed and looking forward to a rare day out. But the next morning the phone rang, and I was asked to stand by, as Howard was not well and might not be able to play the Major General that night. I simply could not believe it. So I went to the theatre as usual that evening, and as it happened, Howard did manage to go on, so I spent the whole time standing by all for nothing. So much for my attempt at sightseeing.

Shortly after our return to England we were to play Manchester, opening with *The Gondoliers* on the Monday night. Seeing that it was *Pirates* the following day. Nick and Sheba came up with me for company, and the plan was that we should drive back that night after the show so that I could have a whole day at home. I'd hardly seen anything of my home for so long, and was looking forward to it very much. During that evening there was a knock at the dressing room door, and Bert Newby, our director of productions entered, looking I thought a little shamefaced. I immediately sensed that there was something wrong. He told me that Howard was unable to play the Major General the following night, and would I do it? I was speechless. 'But. Bert – it's nothing to do with me,' I objected, 'it's no longer my part.' I reminded him what had happened on the American tour. 'I know, John,' he replied, 'but the understudy is not prepared, and we do not want him to go on. All I can do is to ask you.' So there was nothing for it – Nick had to get back to London, so we would have to drive down after *Gondoliers* and I'd return to Manchester the following morning to play the Major General that night.

At the end of the week Stanley Knight, our assistant manager, came to see me with some unbelievable information which no organization but the D'Oyly Carte could possibly have devised. Since the role of the Major General was no longer mine I would have to be paid for my performance, and the fee would be – wait for it – THREE POUNDS! After I had recovered from the shock Stanley suggested that I might like a night off instead, and of course I jumped at the opportunity. I simply did not understand how the management could insult me with such a fee.

Talking of Manchester, some years later – after the Saturday night show, a rather frightening incident occurred. Everyone was in their dressing rooms, hurrying to remove their make-up and get changed in order to get a quick drink before the pubs closed at eleven p.m. A lot of laughter and singing was going on, as is quite usual after a show, and suddenly there was a huge explosion, which we all immediately suspected to be an IRA bomb. I was still in my underclothes when it happened, and standing in front of the window, which had frosted glass and bars for security, and looked directly on to the pavement. I was sprayed with broken glass as the window blew in, and literally blown off my feet across to the opposite wall, Sheba landing beside me. We were both very shocked, and almost at once heard police shouting that another bomb was about to go off, and would everyone leave the theatre at once by the front of house exit and not by the stage door. I dressed at the speed of lightning and was hurrying out with poor Sheba when the thought struck me that my brand new car was parked a little way off. I remember having grumbled that no matter how early I arrived at the theatre I never seemed able to get the prime position outside the stage door, but was I glad that night! Most of the cars in the immediate vicinity had been damaged by the blast, but mine was completely unscathed. The only strange thing was that it was no longer in the position I had left it, but farther down the street. It was still locked up, and I puzzle to this day how it could have got there, and how it was moved without any keys.

All the dressing room windows at the Opera House were on the same side of the building, and every one had been broken, but miraculously nobody had a scratch on them. Ken Sandford, who was always one of the first to get changed, came out of the stage door and was practically blown under one of the cars, but emerged quite unhurt. The bomb was not intended for the theatre, we were told later, but for the law courts, which were close by.

I was feeling pretty miserable, because Saturday night was when I usually dashed home for a brief weekend, but nobody was allowed to go to their vehicles until further notice, so it was back to my digs with Sheba. At about three am I phoned the police and was given the OK to collect my car, though it was by then too late to set off for London. However, the fact that nobody was hurt was the most important thing. Nothing else really mattered. When we got to the theatre the following Monday all the windows had been replaced. In the jar of removing cream on my dressing table I found a large dagger-shaped splinter of glass – how easily that might have struck me – I shuddered at the thought. What a lucky escape we had all had.

In 1979 news broke of a forthcoming tour of Australia and New Zealand, and my heart sank. I really did not want to travel so far from home, especially as it wasn't all that long since we had returned from the USA. I hated the thought of going away again so soon, and for such a long time – the projected tour was to last seventeen weeks.

When the time came for my interview with Mr Lloyd I said as much, and he tried to persuade me in his usual manner, inferring that the tour would simply not go ahead without me. He put his arm round my shoulder, but I shook it off. 'Don't do that!' I said crossly. 'Apparently my performance of the Major General not so long ago which incidentally saved the show, was only worth three pounds!' Freddie could not but be embarrassed, and I added, 'If you're as short of money as that, you can have it back!'

Did I go? Yes, being me, I gave way under pressure, as I had done before. But I believe that disillusionment with the company, with the management, and indeed with certain of my colleagues was beginning to dawn upon me, after so many years of happiness. I remembered the times I had asked for a day off when we were moving house – always I would be called in at the last moment for some minor rehearsal or other, leaving Nick to do everything. Then there were the two occasions when I had missed a rehearsal, once when I was asked to travel to one of the tour venues early, for just half an hour or so (I missed that one on purpose) and another that I forgot completely. I received two stern letters from the management reprimanding me for this. They must have forgotten the times I had stepped in to help them when I needn't have done so.

I always hated flying, and the journey to Sydney took the best part of twenty-five hours including stops at Bombay, and I believe Bernai. Most people left the plane then, but I remained to try to get some sleep, for I could never relax during the flight. It was about nine am local time when we arrived in Sydney, and the whole company apart from myself and Derek Glynne, who was responsible for the tour, left for Canberra, our first venue. At six pm I was still in the VIP lounge, trying to catch up with some sleep on what seemed to me a very sumptuous sofa. I hadn't much idea what was happening – I'd probably been told, but was far too weary to take it in. Derek was engaged in talking business, but eventually he came to tell me that we were to fly to Melbourne to do some publicity, most importantly the Don Laine television show, which was very big in Australia at that time. When we finally reached the studio in Melbourne my Sir Joseph Porter costume was already hanging there in the dressing room, so it was on with the make-up and on to the set. Goodness knows how it went, I was hardly aware of what was going on, so weary and jet-lagged was I. Imagine my horror when I heard that the show had been sold to America, a fact that was proved when I received cheques for the transmissions. What it must have been like, goodness knows, but as long as I didn't have to see it, I didn't care too much. Publicity followed at other cities until I began to feel I was never out of a plane.

At last Derek and I arrived in Canberra to find the company well rested, but me still with my jet lag which I had had no chance to shake off. Our first opera was to be *Iolanthe,* and we were called for rehearsal, which went very well. We wanted the show to be especially good, for there were to be many civic dignitaries present on the opening night. Fraser Goulding, who was conducting, thanked us all and said the principals could go, but he'd just like to keep the chorus for two minutes to tidy up a section in Act I finale. It was nearing one thirty, and the equity representative promptly stood up and said, 'You know you'll be going into overtime, Mr Goulding.' So he had no option but to dismiss them.

Now, I know Equity rules are made to be obeyed, and are often extremely necessary – I've been a member of the union all my working life, still am in fact – but on this occasion the chorus had spent the best part of a week relaxing and enjoying themselves – couldn't they have spared an extra two minutes just this once? Disillusioned, I left the rehearsal room. 'Well, that's it,' I said to Jill Pert. And that was the day I handed in my resignation.

It seemed to me that the 'family feeling' so long associated with the D'Oyly Carte had imperceptibly begun to fade over the years, and it was suddenly brought home to me at that rehearsal. My thoughts went back over the years to all the wonderful people I'd worked with; Valerie Masterson, Gillian Knight and Donald Adams, all of whom had gone on to make names for themselves in grand opera, and farther back still to my days in the chorus and the friends I had made then: Cynthia Morey, Jennifer Toye, Neville Griffiths, Elizabeth Howarth, Eileen Shaw, John Fryatt – all had moved on to Sadler's Wells, Alice Hynd to Covent Garden. Then there were my dear friends who were no longer with us: Alan Styler, John Webley and Jack Habbick. How I missed them all. And Cis Blain and Flo Ewbank who had worked so hard in the wardrobe – they were such characters. Where were the characters of today?

I thought of all those wonderful roles I had played for so long – it would be hard to part from them. But I had realised for some time that in the not too far distant future I would have to relinquish the younger roles – Robin Oakapple in *Ruddigore,* and my beloved Jack Point in *Yeomen* for instance. Then there was Bunthorne – he'd have to go too, before long, I supposed. Perhaps, all in all, it was time for me to leave. My decision had been the right one.

When the company heard I was going, the atmosphere was decidedly cool, and I thought perhaps they feared that the end of the D'Oyly Carte might be on the cards. But why should it be? James Conroy Ward, my understudy, was ready to take over from me, and Alistair Donkin would be principal understudy and play Major General Stanley, as James had done for me. And as it turned out, the D'Oyly Carte Opera Company would continue for a further two and a half years.

My last night in Australia was a sad one. We were in Perth, where there were no house tabs, so that the number of curtain calls was indicated by lights right up at the back of the circle. When these remained constant, another call was indicated. When they twinkled, it was the final curtain call, followed by a blackout, and we could leave the stage. I went to my dressing room, took off my costume and make-up, left the theatre and went back to my hotel.

Farewell, D'Oyly Carte – my raison d'être for the past twenty-eight years. I was now out of work, entirely by my own doing. I little knew then that the next twenty years of a new career was just about to begin.

CHAPTER 16

'I stick to my work till I drop at it.' *(Thespis)*

News travels fast on the theatre grapevine – faster still on the Gilbert and Sullivan equivalent! Almost as soon as I had given in my resignation, work began to come in from various quarters, some of these while I was still in Australia with the company. One of the first was from Norman Meadmore. He was presenting the Gilbert and Sullivan operas at various venues throughout the UK, and he asked me to play Ko-Ko in his production of *The Mikado* at the Barbican. I agreed at once, for the thought of being out of work after so long in regular employment still loomed large in my mind. Here was a chance to go on playing the roles I loved, and to develop them with a freedom hitherto denied me.

I had known Norman for many years, having first met him in March 1952, when he joined the D'Oyly Carte as assistant stage manager to Jerry Stephens. He left the company after about three years, returning briefly in 1957 and finally taking up the post of Stage Director under Bert Newby in 1958. Here Norman remained until 1963, after which time he collaborated with Tom Round and Donald Adams to form their 'Gilbert and Sullivan for All' company. This proved to be a great success, but by the time I left the D'Oyly Carte in 1979 Norman had been presenting his own G&S productions for a number of years, and it was in one of these that I was invited to appear. I continued to work for Norman for some considerable time. but engagements with his company were interspersed with all kinds of other things, which made work extremely interesting and varied. The strict routine I had experienced for twenty-eight years no longer ruled my life. I was probably working just as hard as I had ever done, but now I had the freedom to choose, to select the things I really wanted to do and to turn down offers I considered less interesting, but those were very few.

About a fortnight after I had left the D'Oyly Carte I received the most unexpected phone call from the management. The company were in Nottingham, the show that night was *HMS Pinafore,* and it seemed that both James Conroy-Ward and his understudy, Alistair Donkin, were off sick. Was I free that night, and would I consider playing Sir Joseph Porter? What a situation! I recalled that I had hardly ever been off all the time I had played those roles. Luckily I did happen to have that evening free, so I agreed to do it – and they paid me more than three pounds for my performance this time – I saw to that! It was a strange feeling arriving at the theatre – a weird sensation of déjà vu. Everyone was so pleased to see me, and Ken Sandford said, 'It's like a breath of fresh air, John,' as he shook my hand. Beti Lloyd Jones came to my dressing room before the show just as she had always done, and it seemed for a moment that I had never left. There was an announcement of course before the overture began: 'Ladies and gentlemen, we regret to say that James Conroy-Ward and his understudy are unfortunately indisposed. However, we have been very lucky to find a substitute who is no stranger to Gilbert and Sullivan – Mr John Reed!' The reception which greeted that statement left me deeply moved; the applause was deafening, and of course I could do no wrong that night. And the treatment I received from the management was quite unlike anything I had known before – there was a hotel booked for me, and parking reserved. If they could always have treated their principal artists with that sort of consideration, perhaps things might have been different. Though I can honestly say that I have never had cause to regret the decision I made that day in Australia to hand in my resignation – it was the right thing to do, and exactly the right time to do it.

It wasn't long before some amateur Gilbert and Sullivan societies began to approach me to direct for them, and the first was Harrogate. Joyce Wright had been in charge of productions there for some time, and wanted to give it up, so I managed to fit their rehearsals and performances in with my other work, which was increasing in quantity at a surprising rate. I continued to direct for Harrogate for a number of years, and after a performance one night, some committee members from the Halifax society who had been to see the show, came round to ask if I would direct for them, and I agreed. Looking back at this time, I really don't know how I managed to fit everything in, but somehow I did.

In 1981 I was approached to do a one-man show, *'A Song to Sing, O'*, based on the career of George Grossmith, to who I am said to bear quite a resemblance. Certainly Bridget thought so, and she gave me a very nice photograph of him to mark the occasion. The show, appropriately enough, was to be at the Savoy, and to run for just one week from April 8th. It was presented by Bridget D'Oyly Carte and Hugh Wontner. Written by Australian Melvyn Morrow, the play takes place in Grossmith's dressing room between matinee and evening performances on the day of his last appearance with the D'Oyly Carte. The date is August 17th 1899. There were twenty-four musical items, so I was kept busy, popping behind a screen to change bits of costume and props. There were songs from the G&S operas, naturally, but also some delightful numbers by Grossmith himself, the most well-known being 'See Me Dance the Polka'. I enjoyed the performances, but oh – what a lonely affair is a one-man show! No fellow artists to chat with, no sounds of singers warming up in their dressing rooms, and worst of all, no tuning up of the orchestra to provide that initial excitement to which I had so long been accustomed.

Immediately prior to this show I had been playing Ko-Ko in Malta for Norman Meadmore, and soon afterwards I would be off to the USA, for demands for my services there were steadily escalating. 1982 saw the tragic demise of the D'Oyly Carte Opera Company, and I was invited to do some guest performances during that final season at the Adelphi Theatre – what a pity it was not at the Savoy. As soon as I started to rehearse for these it was as if I had never been away, in spite of the fact that I had left two and a half years previously, and had met crowds of new people and played with different artists in many countries. Friends popped into my dressing room to say, 'Good luck' and Beti of course came to fix my collar as usual – (the opera was *Iolanthe).* It was like a flashback in a film. As soon as I made my entrance I relaxed, completely comfortable, for here I was – back with my `family'.

The matinee on the very last day, 27th February, 1982, was *HMS Pinafore,* and I was to sing Sir Joseph Porter. So in actual fact I did the final performance ever by the D'Oyly Carte of a Gilbert and Sullivan opera, as did David Mackie, who was conducting that afternoon. The show in the evening was to be a farewell concert of miscellaneous items, to give everyone a chance to take part, with Fraser Goulding conducting.

And what a marathon that last evening was! So many numbers from all the operas – in chronological order, apart from that wonderful overture from – *The Yeomen of the Guard* which opened the proceedings. 'Rataplan' from *Cox and Box* followed, and *Thespis* was represented by the girls' chorus from *Pirates,* 'Climbing over rocky mountain' from which indeed it had originally come. After that I sang the Judge's song from *Trial,* and so it went on. Everyone was involved, all the principals were featured, and the men's chorus in the Entrance of the Peers from *Iolanthe* had never sounded more majestic. My other contributions to the programme were 'So go to him and say to him', the duet from *Patience* with Patricia Leonard, and the trio from *Iolanthe,* 'If you go in' with John Ayldon and Geoffrey Shovelton.

The end was indescribably sad. I lost count of the number of curtain calls – they went on and on. Finally we all turned to one another, there were emotional hugs all round and we walked quietly from the stage. The D'Oyly Carte had been confined to history, leaving both cast and audience in a state of bewilderment and disbelief. Over a century of tradition had disappeared at a stroke. But the curtain was not brought down at the end of that last performance; it remained raised. As we made our sad exit into the wings we saw big husky stage hands in tears, carried away by the emotional tension of that unforgettable evening. But one thing we shall always remember-the curtain never fell on the D'Oyly Carte Opera Company.

So much for the D'Oyly Carte. But what of Gilbert and Sullivan? As we have seen, they live on, and sure enough on October 16th of that same year I did the first of four weekly concerts for BBC Radio 2 under the title of 'Gilbert and Sullivan at the Barbican'. I scripted the concerts, which each lasted two hours, and consisted of excerpts from various operas, which I introduced and linked. A few of my old friends took part, including Pamela Field and Michael Wakeham, but most of the others were from Sadler's Wells or Covent Garden – fine singers such as Michael Langdon, John Lawrenson, Anne Collins and Sandra Dugdale amongst them. But though I am the first to admire artists like this, I always feel that there was a certain style acquired by members of the D'Oyly Carte that seems to me to have come right down the ages from Gilbert and Sullivan themselves. I don't quite know how to describe it – it is an elusive quality that has nothing to do with vocal merits or acting ability. It's just, well, *style.*

Interesting dates with Norman Meadmore's company continued intermittently, and these included a cruise on the QE2, where we did a series of G&S concerts which proved very popular. The thing I remember most about this nautical enterprise was trying to take a curtain call in rather rough conditions. The line-up would start centre stage and suddenly find itself in a heap stage left; the next bow would find us lurching over to stage right. However, I was pleased to find myself unaffected by these conditions – unlike Sir Joseph Porter I did *not* find myself having to 'seek the seclusion that a cabin grants!'

We gradually travelled farther afield with G&S concerts, and I remember a delightful visit to the Virgin Islands, where we arrived in the evening. Our hotel was right on the beach, and it was so hot that we tore off our clothes and waded into the warm sea. But we had competition during our concerts – as soon as we started to sing, a vociferous choir of tree frogs joined in, and we hoped our D'Oyly Carte diction would prevail over all that enthusiastic accompaniment going on in the background!

It was a shock to us all when Norman died suddenly in 1984 and we missed him sadly, but one of his four sons, Andrew, took over at the helm, and the Meadmore enterprise continued. I was acquainted with all Norman's sons, for over the years they had each played the midshipmite in *Pinafore* so, as Sir Joseph Porter I had patted them all on the head in turn.

One tour took us up the east coast of the USA and I met again some delightful people, Mr and Mrs Lahey and their family, whom I had first had the pleasure of meeting in Boston a number of years previously when I was still with the D'Oyly Carte. There were four little boys and I remember them sitting, round-eyed, in a row on the sofa in my dressing room as I talked to them about the operas. I had a number of brown bears sitting on my table, and the smallest asked why they were there. I explained that they were supposed to bring good luck to people in the theatre. Silver dollars, too, were lucky, and if you were given one it meant that you would come back to America. The family were in again to the show on the Saturday and the smallest shyly handed me a small parcel. I thanked him, and his father said, 'I think he wants you to open it.' So I did, and I found it contained a brown bear with a silver dollar. I was so touched at this, and hoped I'd see them again some time, though I didn't think this would be very likely. So it was an unexpected pleasure when we did meet again on my tour with the Meadmore group. The small boy was now a young man, and he handed me a parcel, just as he had done before. I opened it and discovered another brown bear – this time carrying a sack full of silver dollars! I thought how wonderful it was of him to remember what we had talked about such a long time ago when he was just a small boy, but then Americans are like that. I never spent those silver dollars – I have them still.

Another tour of Meadmore concerts took us to Holland, where we did sixteen one-night stands – I shudder to think of that now. And there were many more engagements in the UK. I remember a *Yeomen* at the Festival Theatre, Chichester, which is almost theatre in the round. This meant quite a lot of re-thinking of the action, and I made my entrance as Jack Point from a vomitorium – what an unpleasant word that is! I learned that it originates from the passageway in an ancient Roman amphitheatre, and I suppose the Chichester theatre is a little like that. There are about four of these entrances there, and I had to time everything very carefully in order to arrive on stage in time. But I believe it was quite an effective way of beginning that scene.

I did a radio interview with Terry Wogan during these years, which was very amusing. He knew quite a bit about the G&S operas, and told me he'd played Antonio in *The Gondoliers* at school. 'Though you needn't mention that when we're on air,' he said. But I did, of course, and he had to admit to it. Our chat ended with the Bell trio from *Pinafore,* in which he participated lustily.

I was invited to Brussels to direct a couple of the operas for the society there which is composed of English and English-speaking European Union employees – *Iolanthe* and *Yeomen,* in which I played Jack Point as well as directing. I also did a music hall there which was an amusing change, singing that marvellous old number 'The Night I appeared as Macbeth' – certainly a departure from my usual repertoire.

But invitations to work in America were starting to come in from all directions. These had to be fitted in somehow, and were soon to play a major part in my exciting new career.

CHAPTER 17

'A wand'ring minstrel I' (*The Mikado*)

I had been surprised at how swiftly the news of my departure from the D'Oyly Carte had spread in the UK, but in no time at all my possible availability began to spark a lot of interest from companies in the USA. I was busy with Norman Meadmore's productions and concerts, and with the Harrogate and Halifax societies, but as offers of work started to come in from America at a surprising rate I now had to make innumerable trips to the States. My life was fast becoming a complicated jigsaw into which the pieces had to be fitted with care and accuracy.

Washington Opera – *Trial by Jury*

My first American engagement was with Washington Opera. Martin Feinstein was the General Director of the company, and he was also Sol Hurok's right hand man. Mr Hurok had arranged many of the D'Oyly Carte's American tours, so they were both obviously aware that I had left the company and might consequently be available. Washington was to put on *Trial by Jury* and wanted me for the Judge and a contract was duly signed. What a production that was – what costumes, and what a set! The bridesmaids were gorgeous, and wore exquisite dresses with bustles, which looked very similar to those in the original production of 1875. The set was beautifully and solidly built, with a bannister rail down which I was able to slide with the greatest of ease, and we were showered with rose petals as I claimed my bride at the end.

But, having come all the way from England, I was not going to be allowed to get away with just playing the Judge. The original *Trial,* presented at the Royalty Theatre, London, had been teamed with an Offenbach operetta, *La Périchole*, and Washington Opera was to do a similar thing, only this time the accompanying piece was to be a lesser-known work, *Monsieur Choufleuri*. Peter Schifter, the director, asked me to play the role of Monsieur Balandard – in French! This would surely be a complete departure from G&S, I thought, and a somewhat daunting challenge. However 'nothing venture , nothing win' so I set about learning the part, and quite enjoyed the novel experience. In fact, members of the audience surprised me by saying that they understood my French better than that of the singer who played the leading role, who actually was a Frenchman! That was probably because my version of the language was very English, being rather of the 'la plume de ma tante' variety.

While I was performing in this double bill at the John F Kennedy Centre, Al Bergeret, the director of the New York Gilbert and Sullivan Players (known as 'NYGASP') and the company's accountant Charlie Pye, turned up to see the show, after which they came round to my dressing room. Would I be interested in playing King Gama in their next production of *Princess Ida*? They always put on their New York productions at Christmas, at the Symphony Space, Broadway, and took them to other towns and cities in the eastern states in the New Year: Boston, Poughkeepsie, Richmond Virginia, Stamford Connecticut etc. All this seemed to fit in well with other dates in my diary, so the latter part of 1981 and the beginning of '82 were now taken up with work in the States.

I enjoyed my visits to New York. Al Bergeret was a remarkable man, he directed the productions, conducted the shows, built the scenery, in fact, he turned his hand to anything. Nick and I were on our way to the airport one day, on our way to catch a flight home, when we caught sight of Al driving a truck full of scenery! Of course, he had plenty of assistants, he couldn't have coped without them, but he was the king pin around which everything revolved.

Most of Gilbert's dialogue can be understood and appreciated by American audiences, so it remains – as it should – unaltered. But there are the odd references which are incomprehensible except to the British – 'a parliamentary Pickford' is one of them, and has to be changed. We also had to see what could be done with 'sat a gee' – the unlikely rhyme to 'strategy' in the Major General's song in *Pirates,* as it, too, seemed to mystify the audience. Americans don't seem to indulge in 'baby talk' with their children, so would certainly never have heard of a 'gee-gee'. It was decided that when the Major General mutters, 'strategy, strategy, strategy' trying in vain to find a rhyme for it, he should add in anguished tones, 'Oh, my God!' Whereupon a celestial voice boomed out from above, 'Yes? Why not try 'sat a gee?' 'But what does it mean?' asks the Major General. 'Why, rode a horse' booms God. 'Oh, oh, I will,' replies the Major General, 'Thank you.' 'You're welcome,' says God, 'Have a nice day!' He would sometimes add, 'Merry Christmas!' or 'Happy New Year!' according to the season. I'm not quite sure what WSG would have thought of that, but the American audiences loved it. Actually, I tried it out with the Manx Gilbert and Sullivan Society when I was directing there, and a member of the audience got up and walked out – she thought it was blasphemous! I certainly hadn't intended that.

While all this was going on, it seemed that the Music Department of the University of Colorado, in Boulder, had decided to turn their attention to Gilbert and Sullivan instead of their usual grand opera.

They wrote to the D'Oyly Carte office to ask for advice concerning the appointment of a director, 'John Reed's recently left the company,' they were told. 'He may well be interested,' The university approached me and I agreed to go to Boulder to direct their production of *Trial, Cox and Box* and a one-act Offenbach operetta, which was to take place in the summer of 1981. I little knew then that I would be returning there every summer for the next twelve years – or, for that matter, that I would be in New York every winter for almost as long. I directed nearly all of the Gilbert and Sullivan operas in Boulder, and once went on as a rather small policeman in *Pirates,* when one of the lads was off. This proved to be rather embarrassing, as the audience were all laughing at me instead of at the Sergeant, which hadn't been my intention at all. I also directed a production of *Orpheus in the Underworld* for them, which provided enormous scope for my powers of imagination, and great fun was had by all. The first time I went to Boulder I remember arriving at Denver airport alone, looking round, wondering, 'How will anyone recognise me?' I needn't have worried. In no time Professor Jackson and several others who had come with him were crowding round, shaking hands and giving me a warm welcome. 'However did you pick me out?' I asked. They smiled, 'We knew you by your clothes,' they said. And I saw at once what they meant. Everyone else was wearing jeans and very informal clothes, and there was I, rather smart, but looking very, very English.

Engagements in the USA continued to increase in number, and fitting them all in, together with work in England, became more and more complicated. Nick was continuing to run the hotel in Bournemouth, where business during the summer season was very good, but during the winter when things slowed down he would close the hotel and come with me to the States. I looked forward to that, for he was an invaluable help to me as well as being a great companion. He would sit in at rehearsals and take notes, and I could ask him to keep an eye on the chorus while I concentrated on the principals. With all the experience gained working at the Savoy, Nick was able to give valuable advice on lighting my productions, and on performance nights he would even help with make-up, if needed. Another important thing, – he would coach the cast in pronunciation, helping them to tone down their long American vowels and adopt the shorter English ones. They were very keen to get this right. In addition to all this he had the necessary business experience which would prove invaluable to me as my work load increased – negotiating contracts, checking travel arrangements, obtaining visas, ensuring that accommodation was suitable, making sure that a car was available for our use, and very often being the chauffeur as well! Nick also actually took part in two of the NYGASP productions; as Bunthorne's solicitor in *Patience* and the Lord Chancellor's trainbearer in *Iolanthe.*

Nicholas Kerri and John Reed together, *Trial by Jury.*

Many American companies, discovering that I was already in the country, would contact me for a concert or a performance, which saved them paying a separate fare from England. The list of dates is mind-boggling, and I sometimes can't believe how I managed to cope with it all. The idea of leaving the D'Oyly Carte in order to spend more time at home became an impossible dream, but I did love what I was doing, the delightful people I met, and all the wonderful memories which I treasure to this day.

Washington Opera invited me to return in 1982 to play Menelaus in their production of *La Belle Hélène,* so it was back to Offenbach again. I was becoming quite an expert in the field of French operetta, this time fortunately in English. I enjoyed the experience very much, though going off in a balloon which took me up into the flies, where I had to wait until the interval to be lowered back to stage level, was rather daunting. There I had to stay, dying for a cup of tea and watching the rest of the cast far below, looking like a swarm of ants, and all rushing off to their dressing rooms.I enjoyed the freedom of Offenbach – one had to get the words as accurate as possible, of course, but there was always the happy knowledge nobody was sitting in the stalls with a libretto, ready to point out any tiny verbal discrepancy!

With Jean Stapleton in Washington

The following year, 1983, I was with in New York with NYGASP when I was invited again to Washington, this time to take part in a gala concert to raise funds for the opera company's next season. It was called 'Washington Opera Follies' and a host of celebrities had given their services. Tickets were $500 each, though I'm glad to say Nick did manage to get a complimentary one. I found myself sharing a dressing room with Douglas Fairbanks Jnr, and tied his bow tie for him. He was a charming and friendly man. My contribution to the programme consisted of the Nightmare Song and the 'Sing booh to you – pooh,

pooh to you' duet from *Patience* with Jean Stapleton, a very well-known actress who was currently appearing in the television series *All in the Family,* the American equivalent of our *Till Death us do Part*. The second half of the programme began with the overture to *Patience,* followed by my song, after which Jean sang 'Silvered is the Raven Hair', then our duet completed the G&S section. Jean was a delightful person and we got on like a house on fire. We only had one rehearsal, but she certainly knew her stuff, and had a good singing voice, too. It was no doubt a great surprise for the audience to see her doing something so different from her usual character work. Some years after this, she was playing in *Arsenic and Old Lace* in New York and suggested that we might do something together, but her play went out on tour, so the proposed venture never materialised.

But, back to the gala concert. Among the illustrious participants were the famous cellist Mstislav Rostropovich, Tammy Grimes, several well-known American actors, and the great Ethel Merman. She was a friend of Jean's, and I was taken to her dressing room to meet her. She had been very ill – just out of hospital, in fact – and looked a shadow of her former self, but insisted on doing the show, returning to hospital afterwards. I shall never forget standing in the wings to watch her. She hardly looked fit to go on, but as soon as she stepped on stage something magical happened, and the great Ethel Merman, star of so many unforgettable Hollywood musicals, suddenly took over. 'There's no Business like Show Business' rang out with as much strength and panache as ever, and the audience gave her the tremendous reception she deserved. I really don't know how she did it. She made a grand exit at the end and collapsed into our arms. I have an idea that her appearance at the gala concert may have been her last, and I am proud to have had the privilege of meeting her.

After so many years in the D'Oyly Carte, where there were no stars and where we were constantly reminded that no member of the company was indispensable, it was strange but not unpleasant to be given the VIP treatment I enjoyed in America. For the concert in Washington we were given a penthouse suite at the Watergate Hotel with every luxury imaginable, and a stretch limousine to take us to the theatre, which was only a block or so away. A far cry from the old touring days!

During one of my visits to Washington I was asked to entertain at a big dinner for judges and attorneys – it was at the Four Seasons restaurant, I believe. I remember circulating among the tables regaling them all with the legally-inspired numbers from the operas; 'When I went to the Bar as a very Young Man, 'The Law is the True Embodiment', the Judge's Song from *Trial* etc. It was certainly an unusual assignment, but there's no doubt about it, you can always find something from the Gilbert and Sullivan operas to suit any occasion.

The D'Oyly Carte were the first company to perform at the new Dorothy Chandler Theatre in Los Angeles, and I was interested to return there a number of years later to sing the part of the Lord Chancellor in *Iolanthe* with the Los Angeles Master Chorale. They were a choral group, so it was to be a concert rather than a performance, but of course that wouldn't do for me – I was soon directing the proceedings. In no time I had some of them in costume, with a few props, arranged some moves and introduced a little choreography. So much more interesting than just standing and singing. They must have thought so too, for I was invited to return the following year to do the same thing with *Pirates*.

One night I came out of the Dorothy Chandler Theatre and went to a nearby restaurant to meet friends, and as I was going in, I heard a great round of applause. I turned round to see who it was for, then realised with much embarrassment that it was for *me!* I could never get used to that sort of thing – it just wouldn't have happened at home. But Americans are so much more extrovert than we are, and express their feelings in a more uninhibited way. It's really rather endearing.

We stayed in Bunker Hill, a very opulent block of apartments with a swimming pool, and a convenient supermarket below, to which we could easily pop down for anything we needed. I remember calling at the drugstore opposite the theatre one day and chatting to the assistant, who asked me if I was on holiday in LA. 'No, I'm working – at the theatre,' I replied. I suppose it was my English accent which prompted him to ask, 'Are you John Reed?' 'Yes,' I said, that's me.' He told me of an eminent doctor who came in regularly. 'He talks of nothing but you,' he said. 'He'd love to meet you. His name's Warren Austin, and he's staying at Bunker Hill.' 'Well, so are we,' I said, and we did meet him and his charming wife, and became very friendly. He had been the physician to the Duke and Duchess of Windsor, and was, I suppose, very wealthy, owning flats in the Barbican and property in Chichester. We found them a delightful couple.

I was still directing for the Harrogate and Halifax societies in between all these American commitments, and was beginning to realise that it was pointless to continue having a home in Bournemouth which I hardly ever saw. As soon as I got back from America I was off up north – so why not move up there to live? After all, I could travel to the States just as easily from there as from Bournemouth. More importantly, I was beginning to realise that I needed someone to look after my professional affairs full time, and who better than Nick to do this? So it was arranged, the hotel was sold and in 1988 we moved into our present house in Halifax, then promptly left for the States!

CHAPTER 18

'Let us fly to a far-off land . . .' *(The Sorcerer)*

When I look back at those busy post-D'Oyly Carte days it seems that a lot of our time was spent in aeroplanes, and to one who hates flying it proves how much I must have loved my work! Nick and I were always amazed during our brief spells back in the UK when friends asked, 'Have a good holiday?' It was a case of arriving at the destination airport, transferring to the hotel, being escorted to see the theatre and rehearsal room, possibly doing a radio or television interview, having something to eat and going to bed. Rehearsals would follow every day after that. Even the flight time was utilised, for there were always last minute things to do, rehearsal schedules to check and production details to discuss. It was a busy but fulfilling period of my life.

As the eighties progressed, I continued to receive offers of work in places we had not visited before: Salt Lake City, Louisville Kentucky, Dallas, Daytona Beach Florida. The regular dates went on as usual – New York at Christmas, followed by the usual US east coast tour, then the summer season in Boulder, Colorado, and all these were interspersed with concerts and productions at home.

Receiving an honorary degree at the University of Colorado

I particularly enjoyed working at Boulder; music students would arrive from all over the States for this popular summer season, and they took Gilbert and Sullivan to their hearts. Every time we broke for a cup of tea they would gather round, wanting to know everything I could tell them about the D'Oyly Carte and the Savoy operas. They were so warm and affectionate towards me, hanging on my every word, and a delight to direct. Those visits to Boulder, which spanned thirteen years, were a source of great pleasure and many happy memories.

We were always pleased to return to NYGASP in New York every year, where we made many friends, some of whom we correspond with to this day. One who instantly comes to mind is Keith Jurosko, an excellent Grosvenor to my Bunthorne in NYGASP'S production of *Patience,* and it's always a pleasure to hear his cheery voice on the phone, giving us all the news. I enjoyed working in Al Bergeret's productions, which were excellent, though

I did have slight reservations when I had to do an encore to the Nightmare Song – and what's more, carrying a teddy bear!

At one NYGASP concert 'Dr Ruth', a well-known television 'love doctor', noted for her advice on sex problems came on stage as a publicity stunt to talk about Phyllis and Strephon's love affair. I'd been singing the Lord Chancellor, so I said to her, 'Look, you're a love doctor – well, *I'm* in love with Phyllis, which isn't getting me anywhere. Will *you* marry me?' I suppose she could have sued me for breach of promise after I'd proposed before all those witnesses, but I didn't think of that at the time! Luckily for me she said, 'I'm sorry, but I'm married already!' I breathed a sigh of relief. There was a party afterwards, and Dr Ruth made her way across the room to me. 'John,' she said, 'My husband's away for a while . . . .' Luckily she was joking!

An engagement in 1988 which comes to mind was a concert in Salt Lake City. I had met tenor Michael Ballam in Washington, when I was in *La Belle Hélène* and he was interested in raising money to re-open an old theatre which had subsequently been through hard times as a cinema and a dance hall. It was certainly in a dreadful state, for the stage had been bricked up, and the whole place was derelict. It seems that some wonderful old Victorian backcloths were discovered when the stage was finally revealed, and I like to think that our G&S concert helped to raise some funds towards the grand old theatre's reinstatement. The restoration venture was apparently a great success, as the theatre is now a large and important venue, able to accommodate major opera and ballet companies – and I find my name is still on the board.

Another unusual date was at an old Indian theatre in Albequerque, New Mexico, where I did three chaotic concerts – or rather, getting them organised was chaotic, though the performances themselves turned out to be an enormous success. Professor

Jackson, from Boulder, arranged it, and we were to do *Trial by Jury* plus various excerpts from the operas. I was alarmed when I arrived to find the chorus provided knew very little of *Trial,* and not that much of anything else, so we had to improvise like mad. I remember telling them, 'Oh, just say, 'Here comes the Judge" as they couldn't possibly learn the chorus 'All hail, great Judge' in time. But in spite of these drawbacks we got together three amazingly good concerts which were very enthusiastically received.

Doing *The Yeomen of the Guard* at Louisville, Kentucky, was particularly enjoyable for me when I discovered that Mary Smith, a delightful soprano who had played Helen in *La Belle Hélène* with Washington Opera, was to play Elsie. She had both the voice and the looks to go with it, and was a joy to work with.

Another production of *The Yeomen of the Guard* which I was to direct was for Cleveland opera, in a very large theatre seating, I believe, four thousand. Facilities were perfect in every way, but I got the idea that the stage manager rather disapproved of the fact that we were to do mere Gilbert and Sullivan when the company had always performed grand opera. Everything I did provoked the remark, 'Oh, we did that in *Tosca',* and every prop I asked for received the reply, 'Oh, yes, we've got one from *'Tosca'* I had the idea that in one scene the off-duty Warders would enter, stand their halberds in a barrel and sit informally round a refectory-type table with tankards of beer. 'I shall need a large table,' I said, 'and before you say anything, I don't want one from bloody *Tosca!'* Everyone laughed, and the stage manager was obviously embarrassed, especially as all the powers that be were sitting in the stalls, but he never referred to *Tosca* again.

There was nothing snobbish about the singers, however, for although they had sung exclusively in grand opera, they were very much intrigued with Gilbert and Sullivan. Also, they were unused to speaking dialogue, particularly with an English accent, so were keen to learn. Marian Pratniki, a wonderful Dame Carruthers, would not even begin to rehearse each day until she had given me a hug, and as she was a pretty large lady I nearly got lost in the folds! When our stage manager saw how everyone was enjoying themselves and loving Gilbert and Sullivan he changed his attitude. There was obviously more to these 'comic operas' than he had realised. I was glad about this, for I like to be on good terms with everybody and have a happy company.

When I went to play the Duke of Plaza-Toro in *The Gondoliers* for the Lyric Opera of Dallas we were invited to stay in the beautiful home of Overton and Suzette Shelmyre, who were great supporters of the company. The house was built in colonial style and stood in extensive grounds with a lake. We had the most luxurious accommodation with fourposter beds, and I particularly remember the wonderful black cook who served our breakfast. 'Ham and eggs? Praise the Lord!' she would say with a beaming smile. 'Tea or coffee? Hallelujah!' Grandfather Reed would certainly have approved. I was enjoying myself one day, lying back in a boat as we floated across the lake, trailing my hand in the water. 'There are aligators in this lake,' our host remarked casually. My hand was out of that water before you could say 'Jack Point.' The next thing we spotted was a large snake curled up on the bank, so decided to keep away from the lake in future – Texan wild life was not for us!

Daytona Beach, Florida, turned out to be one of our favourite venues, and it was there that I was invited, once again, to direct *The Yeomen of the Guard*. It seems that Americans are particularly keen on the more English of the G&S operas, so *Yeomen* and *Iolanthe* are always very popular. Auditions to appear in Daytona were held in New York, and the whole cast was highly talented in all branches of theatre. It was here that I met Gary Biggles – one of the best Jack Points I have ever worked with. When we first met he was so nervous that he was almost in tears, and I could see at once that he possessed the sensitivity which is so necessary for that role. He was absolutely splendid, and it was wonderful to work with him, as it was with the whole cast. As at Boulder, none of them knew anything about Gilbert and Sullivan, but they were keen to learn. Every rehearsal was like a master class; I might dismiss the chorus and keep the principals to go through some scene or other, but did the chorus go? They certainly did not. They would sit round quietly, drinking it all in, hanging on my every word. If I'd taught them a dance step I would see them practising at every opportunity until they'd got it right. At the next rehearsal it would be perfect. Incidentally, there is an object lesson here for many amateur societies. It is extremely frustrating to have to cope with the constant noise and chatter which seems to be the norm at rehearsals, the annoying absences when you are trying to rehearse a certain scene, and the fact that many members have very often not given a thought to the production since they last met. Of course, there are many dedicated amateur performers, and it is not to them I speak. It is to the many others, who would do well to 'list and learn' if they wish to reach the standard required for a performance that the audience pay to see.

The *Yeomen* set was beautifully built, with leaded windows and a dramatically lit Tower. Every detail was carefully worked out; there were torches on the back wall filled with a meticulously calculated amount of oil so that they would dim and go out at exactly the right moment. Now, that's what I call precision.

We went to Tulsa, Oklahoma three times, from 1991 to 1993, and I directed *The Yeomen of Guard* (once again!), *The Gondoliers* and *The Mikado* at a splendid university theatre. Nick and I were taken to see an open-air performance of Rodgers and Hammerstein's *Oklahoma* one evening, and had just found our seats and sat down when an announcement was made: 'Ladies and gentlemen, we have John Reed in the audience tonight' I suddenly found myself, highly embarrassed, in a spotlight, and had to stand up and acknowledge the applause that followed. The same thing had happened to me years before, when I was at a concert at the Hollywood Bowl with Sol Hurok, and currently playing Los Angeles with the D'Oyly Carte. Both times I was amazed to be singled out like that, not realising how well known I had become in the world of American theatre. Nothing like that would ever have happened in England.

We enjoyed Tulsa very much, in spite of the frequent threat of tornados – or 'twisters' as they are called. I was watching television one night and heard a warning that one was approaching, then saw to my horror that it was to be in our immediate area – the picture showed nearby streets. I shouted to Nick, who was upstairs in bed, and he came rushing down. I don't know what I thought we could do – get in a cupboard, I suppose, but luckily for us it passed by harmlessly and we breathed a sigh of relief.

We were very touched when the Tulsa Gilbert and Sullivan Society presented us with a silver plaque mounted on a wooden base shaped like the state of Oklahoma, bearing this inscription:

'Presented to John Reed OBE and Nicholas Kerri on the 8th July 1993
With thanks, appreciation for their work in presenting the Genius of
Gilbert and Sullivan to American audiences and, in particular, for
their triumphant collaboration with the Gilbert and Sullivan Society
of Tulsa (1991-1993) Right good captains and good judges too
Let them be celebrated, cultivated. but never underrated

Bernard Everett, Her Britannic Majesty's Consul General'

It was a very nice gesture, and the plaque hangs above the mantelpiece, reminding us of some extremely happy times. It fits in well with all the G&S characters which fill the high shelf around our living room. They are a combined effort by myself and Nick; I modelled them in clay and he painted them, taking infinite care to get the colours of the costumes exactly authentic. As well as the plaque, we received the Freedom of the City of Tulsa from the Mayor, Roger A Randle, being formally assured 'that we held a place of honor and high esteem in the hearts and minds of the citizens of Tulsa, Oklahoma'. We were indeed honoured. When we left Daytona Beach after that successful *Yeomen I* had accepted an invitation to return the following year to direct *Iolanthe,* and had already begun to devise some new ideas for the production. I thought it might be effective for the Peers to enter in morning dress, each carrying a small case, and accompanied by valets, bearing their robes, On cue the valets would array them in their full glory, coronets would appear from the small cases and be placed on their heads, then away the Peers would sweep, into that majestic march. I remember mentioning this idea to one of the men, who then looked very puzzled. 'What's a 'morning' suit?' he asked. I laughed – apparently such things did not exist in America, so I drew a sketch to show him.

Well, all this would have been great fun, but alas – it was not destined to happen. Little did I realise that I had directed my last American production, for at this point Mother Nature intervened and said 'Enough!' Soon after we returned home I became ill and had to spend a week in hospital – unheard of for *me* – on account of a suspected heart condition. Luckily this was soon sorted out and I was pretty well back to normal, but we both felt that perhaps it was time to end this globe-trotting marathon and stay in one place for a while!

But of course, being me, I still had to have my finger in the Gilbert and Sullivan pie, and was soon continuing with local societies. Another thing happened just about then – two Gilbert and Sullivan enthusiasts, Ian Smith and his son Neil, decided that it might be an interesting idea to start an annual G&S festival, to promote and expand interest in the operas. The charming Opera House in Buxton, designed by Frank Matcham, was suggested as a possible venue, so Nick and I went to see it. It was indeed just right for such an event, and in August 1994 the first Festival took place and has continued ever since. I was appointed President and have given my services many times, directing, giving master classes or talking about the operas and the D'Oyly Carte.

My two careers with Gilbert and Sullivan – twenty-eight years with the D'Oyly Carte and a further fourteen as a freelance performer and director – have been an endless source of pleasure and fulfilment, and I cannot think of a more wonderful way of spending my life. I often look back across the years and imagine what it might have been like if I had left the company to try my luck elsewhere, outside the confines of the Savoy Operas. But the few times I considered making the break I couldn't quite bring myself to do it. It may have been weakness – 'but the weakness was so strong' – so I stayed, and to be honest, I've never regretted it. The ties of Gilbert and Sullivan held me fast. And wherever I went, whatever new group of people I met, and in whatever country, I was never a stranger. The mutual love and enthusiasm for the Savoy Operas broke the ice immediately and made us friends from the start.

I think the most important words ever addressed to me in the whole of my life were those spoken by Frederick Lloyd after my audition for the D'Oyly Carte way back in 1951:

'We want you Mr. Reed. How soon can you join us?'

And to think I nearly refused!

John Reed

16993719R00102

Printed in Poland
by Amazon Fulfillment
Poland Sp. z o.o., Wrocław